# Unremarkable to Extraordinary

"I have watched Jeremy's journey for many years, and he has been the epitome of what success looks like in this entrepreneurial world. Jeremy is someone I greatly admire because he has effectively executed the most powerful strategy you could ever have for personal growth... connecting with power.

Jeremy has learned directly from some of the greatest minds how to create his own success and he is someone I wholeheartedly believe has the intention to help others accomplish the same level of success. This is a book that should be on every entrepreneur or aspiring entrepreneur's shelf."

**Manuel Suarez,**
CEO
AGM Marketing

"I love what Jeremy has done with his book...he did exactly what he said he would do; produced a book that is simple to read. A book that is meant to inspire and help people work through personal barriers to reach great heights. Jeremy introduces a diverse group of characters to serve as examples of what passion and dedication can lead to.

If *Unremarkable to Extraordinary* doesn't motivate you to take that first step, nothing will! I encourage you to follow Jeremy's example and jump in."

**Gregg Sturdevant**
Major General, USMC ( Retired)
President/ CEO, Mission Critical Leadership Solutions

"As an athlete, coach and author, I've been interviewed more times than I can remember. My conversation with Jeremy however, stands out because of the nature of the questions. It's so much more enjoyable for me when there's a level of understanding that allows for deeper thought, particularly with regard to foundational concepts. If you look at the chapters within the book, these are universal themes, and they apply to every one of us who aspires to be great."

**Duff Gibson,**
Bestselling Author
Canadian Olympic Gold Medalist

"Extraordinary claims require extraordinary evidence and *Unremarkable to Extraordinary* has both! Phenomenal book that will take you from *Unremarkable to Extraordinary*. Jeremy's book helps ordinary people go to extraordinary. Don't miss out on lessons from the classiest podcaster and creator in the known Universe!"

**Dr. Brian Keating**
Professor of Physics
University of California, San Diego

"Building an extraordinary life requires inspiration. Jeremy tells some great stories that are sure to inspire anyone looking to make their mark on the world."

**Brian Scudamore**
Bestselling author of *BYOB: BUILD YOUR OWN BUSINESS, BE YOUR OWN BOSS* and Founder & CEO of 1-800-GOT-JUNK? and O2E Brands

"Having known Jeremy for several years, I know the value he provides. If you are looking to have an extraordinary life, it takes action. *Unremarkable to Extraordinary* has stories and life experiences from those that have taken action to achieve high levels of success so that you can apply the same concepts they did."

**Phillip Stutts**
Founder,
Win Big Media

"Jeremy really understands what it takes to be an extraordinary entrepreneur. And it is not for the faint of heart. *Unremarkable to Extraordinary* shares great stories, terrific inspiration and actionable tips to help anyone become extraordinary too. Read *Unremarkable to Extraordinary!*"

**Kara Goldin**
Founder & Former CEO of Hint, Inc
Author of *Undaunted*.

"Having access to learn and listen to some of the most successful people in their fields has given Jeremy a unique and powerful perspective on living life to the fullest. That perspective is evident in *Unremarkable to Extraordinary*. The true life lessons and personal stories shared throughout this book show that anyone, ANYONE can live an extraordinary life no matter their circumstances. The pervasive question is: have you reached your potential? This book is like a roadmap to assist you on that journey by providing you guideposts and real world examples of those who have achieved the extraordinary. It's time to start your adventure."

**James Barbour**
Award Winning Broadway Star
Best Selling Author & Keynote Speaker

# UNREMARKABLE TO
# EXTRA
# ORDINARY

## IGNITE YOUR PASSION TO GO FROM PASSIVE OBSERVER TO CREATOR OF YOUR OWN LIFE

### JEREMY RYAN SLATE

# Unremarkable to Extraordinary

Ignite Your Passion to go from Passive Observer to Creator of Your Own Life

Published in New York, New York, by Morgan James Publishing. Morgan James is a trademark of Morgan James, LLC. www.MorganJamesPublishing.com

Proudly distributed by Ingram Publisher Services.

**Morgan James BOGO™**

A **FREE** ebook edition is available for you or a friend with the purchase of this print book.

_____

CLEARLY SIGN YOUR NAME ABOVE

**Instructions to claim your free ebook edition:**
1. Visit MorganJamesBOGO.com
2. Sign your name CLEARLY in the space above
3. Complete the form and submit a photo of this entire page
4. You or your friend can download the ebook to your preferred device

ISBN 9781636980560 paperback
ISBN 9781636980577 ebook
Library of Congress Control Number:
2022945823

Morgan James is a proud partner of Habitat for Humanity Peninsula and Greater Williamsburg. Partners in building since 2006.

Get involved today! Visit: www.morgan-james-publishing.com/giving-back

# Acknowledgements

I want to thank Karin Greene for believing in me and the mission I had with my podcast. You gave me that first job to pay the bills when all my other exploits had failed.

To my wife, Brielle, you believed in me when I didn't believe in myself and have supported my dreams, even when early on, you were the one paying the bills.

To David Brier, your guidance in the world of branding has been what I have needed every step of the way. I would not truly be where I am now had I not known how important *"The Art of Differentiation"* is.

To Dr. Jason Dean, you gave me the courage to find my true voice and embrace my mission, not someone else's.

To Jesse Krieger for believing in this book and pushing me to write it.

To Edwin Dearborn, you helped me find my voice in the middle of this writing when I almost gave up.

To the nearly one thousand people I have interviewed on my podcast, though I would have liked to include everything single one of you, it was just not possible. You have helped me more than you will ever know.

To the millions of listeners of my podcast, *Create Your Own Life*, without you, none of this is possible. You have given me license to speak to the world, and I am eternally grateful to you.

# Contents

# Foreword

In business, shrinkage is a big problem.

Let's face it: entrepreneurship is not for the faint-hearted.

Nor is it for those who simply want to show up without also having the goal of leaving an indelible mark on those they serve, whether they be colleagues, protégés, or clients.

As business legend Tom Peters said, "You can't shrink your way to greatness." And this is one of the qualities I love about Jeremy, whom I have known for many years now.

Jeremy loves to serve.

And he has always exhibited that quality, from the first time we connected to the first time Jeremy had me on his excellent podcast.

He truly listens. And his questions are real and convey a true curiosity and desire to learn.

I've seen Jeremy take this tireless desire to learn (only matched by an insane work ethic and comparably insane workout regimen) and use it to bring out the best in his guests on his podcast.

What's special and unique about Jeremy is he uses this level of interest tirelessly to serve clients of all backgrounds, from international organizations to serial entrepreneurs and authors, to elevate their impact in the world.

This is why Jeremy is perfectly poised to write about courage, being extraordinary, overcoming failure, and every other real-world challenge every entrepreneur encounters in *Unremarkable to Extraordinary*.

Jeremy's lived it. He's overcome it. He's embraced it.

And he's interviewed those who have done the same.

And that is what you hold in your hands. A book based on real issues that can be used by real entrepreneurs with real goals and real dreams.

Here's one thing you need to know: I've never wrapped up a phone call with Jeremy where he hasn't asked, "How can I help you?"

This is almost all you need to know.

Anyone who wakes up to serve, and goes to sleep only after they've planned to serve more tomorrow, is someone worth knowing. Or reading about (which is where this book comes in).

Read this book. Apply what's in it.

Your life and career will thank you.

And shrinkage will be a thing of the past.

**David Brier**
Slayer of the Mundane
RisingAboveTheNoise.com

# How to Read this Book

This book comes from research I've carried out in addition to nearly one thousand interviews I've conducted with world-class performers and newsmakers. A lot of what we will talk about comes directly from my conversations with these individuals. Though some of the people I speak to are political, this is not a political book. I may feature people you don't agree with, and my hope is that there is still something you can learn from them. I don't agree with Saul Alinsky politically, but he lays out some brilliant strategies in his book *Rules for Radicals*. After all, we're all people with unique viewpoints on life, and my desire is to learn from them.

If you encounter any words, phrases, or symbols in this book you do not understand, don't blow by them. Take a minute to look them up! It's very important that you understand everything you read in this book. For example, I once encountered a word I didn't understand. I read the sentence and asked myself, "What did I just read?" I re-read the sentence a few times, and it still didn't make any sense. I looked the word up and found out I didn't really know it. If you have that experience, then look it up because I really want you to get the concepts covered in this book.

My goal in writing this is to write something that is well thought out, but simple and easy to understand. Frankly, this book could have been over a thousand pages, but it is meant for maximum impact, not maximum stopping power.

There are several books that I mention in this book. I recommend that you read them, not as a prerequisite, but take a look at them after the fact so that you can get a full conceptual understanding of what I talk about here.

This book is meant to be read straight through, but it is structured in such a way that if you are looking for help in a single area, you can concentrate on that area.

There is a companion to this book called *30 Days to Extraordinary*, which is a 30-day series of the most impactful podcast episodes and lessons you can unpack to move forward in 30 days. You can get this at www.jeremyryanslate.com/extraordinary30.

Throughout the book, you'll encounter four things to help in your journey: *Extraordinary Takeaways, Extraordinary Facts, Extraordinary Stories,* and *Extraordinary Reads.*

**Extraordinary Takeaways:** are the thoughts I'm handing to you on how to receive the stories and messages of the chapter. These are timeless concepts you can return to on those days you're not feeling extraordinary.

**Extraordinary Facts:** are pieces of supporting evidence that I feel will help to enrich your journey to extraordinary.

**Extraordinary Stories:** I'd like to include every story that I've learned over my six-plus years of research, but I just cannot. Extraordinary Stories are interviews I have conducted that you can reference by listening to companion podcast episodes. Each Extraordinary Story gives you a unique entry point to find your extraordinary in 30 days.

**Extraordinary Reads:** included at the end, this is an appendix of books that I have read that have had a huge effect on my own life.

This book is meant not just to inspire you but to show you what is possible and help you see your path for yourself. This book is not meant to be another motivational read, but something to actually help you get past the things you're running into in your life right now. Personally, I've spent a lot of time and money on personal development. You may be in a place where that's not possible right now. This book was created to help you get past whatever your own personal barriers are right now so that you can create the success you want to create. As part of that plan, your own personal development should be a key element in that. If you're interested in what personal development I have concentrated on, I invite you to reach out to me via email at jrs@jeremyryanslate.com.

Personally, I've only concentrated on things that get me results, and I don't mix messages.

Though many authors look at their written work as the solution to readers' problems, I look at this book more as the match to light the flame of your passion. This is by no means a group of personal development exercises I'm selling you. Rather, this book is composed of stories and clear, hard facts.

This book is meant to be an adventure. We will dive deep into the lives of the people I have spoken to and those I have studied. You'll learn very important details about their lives to which you most definitely will see parallels in your own.

We're all human, after all, and there is no scarcity to the success we can all have.

Here's to your adventure into the extraordinary.

**Jeremy Slate**
**November 2021**

# 1. It Takes Courage

*The most courageous act is still
to think for yourself. Aloud.*

—Coco Chanel

The single greatest component to being an extraordinary human being is courage. We are all born with relatively the same elements, such as talent, looks, athleticism, etc. Some have a little more, some have a little less. However, we all have an equal shot to reach our greatness.

Some of the greatest athletes and individuals you've ever heard of are really no different from you. They have the same struggles, they have the same pain, they have the same issues. They have had the courage to reach their greatest possible potential. For one to be great, one must embrace the fear and conquer it.

When I first wrote an early version of this book, I had the courage to realize what I had written was not the impact I was looking to make on the world.

## 🎤 Extraordinary Story

**Marie White:** "Using Your Darkest Hour to Show Others Light"

Marie White experienced one of the worst things that can happen to a parent—she had her child kidnapped. She took this struggle and turned it into strength to help other parents. Since, this interview, after many, many years of searching, Marie's child was returned to her.

*www.jeremyryanslate.com/white*

Where we are and how it started are two very different things. I started writing this manuscript way back in late 2019. I was so excited for the launch of this book.

However, the journey that led me to starting this book through the podcast I started back in 2015 and the version of this book you currently see are two very different things. I've talked to many authors over the years while recording my podcast, and I heard repeatedly that the process of writing is very therapeutic. Not only does it teach you more about your own content; you learn more about who you are.

Well, the interesting part about that is it's very true. I didn't expect for things to change so much, and I also didn't expect the world to change so much. It seems as though we fell into a superstorm; I started the process of writing and better learning who I was and what I thought about things, and then the world shifted into a global pandemic that changed everything we know about life.

The process of writing this book has been much like those memes you see on Instagram, the ones that say how it started and how it's going. First, let's go back to how the process of creating this book started.

## How It Started

In 2011, I wasn't really finding a career path that "fit." I had obtained a master's degree in ancient history, something that was extremely enjoyable but didn't actually qualify me to do a heck of a lot of things. So, when I graduated, I wasn't exactly trained to go out and get a decent job. I was in this weird situation of having a master's degree but not a doctorate degree or teaching degree, which would secure professional-level positions.

I wasn't exactly a dream to hire for any job, but I needed to take action. Being newly graduated, I had a lot of bills and needed to pay for my living expenses.

Through high school and college, I had worked for a painter. I learned how to do everything the old-school way—painting houses by hand with a four-inch brush, and scraping old paint off for hours on end, and doing some crazy things that only painters will do, like hanging from ceilings, walking on wild-angled roofs or, the one that really freaked by dad out, clamping a 2x4 to one leg of a ladder to be able to paint on stairs; maybe it's all those fumes we consumed.

Honestly, that job was the best lesson I ever learned in work ethic. After grad school, I went back to painting houses since I knew it was a way I could at least make money in relation to how hard I was willing to work. That's what I did during the day, then at about 6:00 p.m. I would work as the night manager at a gym until 11:00 p.m. I also worked there all day on Saturday and Sunday and somehow managed to have a social life—be it a very limited one! Somehow, I even had enough time to meet my now wife.

My first step towards a professional career was as a substitute teacher at a high school. That was back in 2012, and I very quickly became a full-time teacher. In private school you don't need a teaching degree in order to teach, so I was able to do what wouldn't have been possible in a public school.

I've always looked young. At 24, I looked like a senior in that high school. Needless to say, my appearance combined with my lack of training made life as a young teacher very difficult. I was left questioning if this would ever be the career I had expected—my goal was to teach at the college level in some capacity—but I embraced where I was for the time being.

In 2012, my mom ended up having a really bad stroke. It was one of the single most difficult events in my life and changed everything from that day forward.

That day made me consider everything I had planned on in life. I was 24, working 80 hours a week for less than $20,000 a year. I wasn't very happy and didn't want to live like this for the rest of my life. Though it was a difficult day, in some ways it was a gift because it made me look very differently at the future.

It took a full year for me to do anything about it. My fiancée had seen a presentation about a network marketing company and mentioned it to me. I had no idea what network marketing was, but I was looking for any way out, and it seemed like a pretty legitimate option.

With no real plan, I called the principal, quit my job, and decided I was going to go full time for this opportunity. I did that for about two years and very quickly burned myself out there as well. I decided the right thing to do was move on, claiming it was the opportunity and not me.

My next step was to sell life insurance, which I was really good at, but I hated the experience of talking about death every single day.

## Extraordinary Story

**Brad Thor:** "Inside the Mind of One of The Greatest Thriller Authors of All Time"

Brad is the author of 20 thriller books and a frequent feature on the *NY Times* bestseller list. Brad had a travel show on public television for years, but it did not really fulfill him. One day, his wife asked him what he'd regret on his deathbed. He realized it would never be writing a novel. That led him down an incredible road to the life he wanted.

*www.jeremyryanslate.com/thor*

I moved on from there to buying products from China and selling them at low cost on Amazon. However, I made the mistake of leaving a promo code on my listing where buyers could get the product for $1 and lost all of my products in less than 20 minutes; I was out of business.

My final option was to teach myself how to build websites from YouTube videos and blog posts and get a job at a friend's marketing company doing just that. I had decided that if this didn't work out, I was going to give up on the dream and just get a career job again. In fact, I had actually started applying for jobs like being a bank teller. It had been a tumultuous several years, and I was close to feeling like I needed security.

I still had this itch, looking for something more, so I started a podcast called *Create Your Own Life* as a hobby. I started it because I had decided at this point, since things hadn't really worked out, I needed more knowledge. I thought the best way to get access to the people I needed would be to have an interview show. I was very right.

Within 30 days, that podcast had 10,000 listens, and I knew I really had something here.

That then led me to starting a company in the podcast space called Command Your Brand. That was way back in 2016. Since then, the small podcast I started has nearly a thousand episodes with millions of people listening to the show. I've been lucky enough to speak to some of the highest performers in the world, but I got to a point where I felt like my content was starting to get stale.

I had started to write this book and honestly, I had about 50,000 words, which is almost a full book, but I held off on publishing it because it just didn't really feel right. It felt very life coachy, which I'm very far from.

Then, in early 2020, the world changed forever. That forced me into the decision to start only talking about things that matter.

## How It's Going

The onset of a global pandemic made it painfully obvious to me that the world we currently live in is nowhere near the world we grew up in. The media is extremely politicized, and every issue, even ones regarding health, have become divisive.

I was someone who was always opinionated in private. I started reading Tom Clancy books at 12, followed by Ron Paul and Rand Paul from a young age. In fact, I had listened to Glenn Beck since before 9/11 when no one knew who it was. I had never really seen myself as a Republican. I lean conservative on economic issues, but I'm pretty liberal on a lot of social issues. Where that puts me on the spectrum, I'm still trying to figure out.

I had never let any of these things seep into my content.

Throughout 2020, I watched the economy crash, riots in our streets, and people in fear of the disease that was spreading like wildfire. The media seemed to operate on selling fear, telling the furthest thing from the truth. As an observer, it seemed to me that they cared more about getting a man out of the White House than actually reporting what was happening so we could make informed decisions as family members, as business owners, and really just as Americans.

## Extraordinary Story

**Dave Rubin:** "Don't Burn This Book: Thinking for Yourself in an Age of Unreason"

Cancel culture has become one of the biggest issues in the public sphere. In actuality, speaking on issues is how we solve things. Dave Rubin, a political pundit, has experienced much of this, and is pointing out why we should not be destroying what we do not agree with. Rather, we should be looking at how we can openly debate it.

*www.jeremyryanslate.com/rubinreport*

I watched my good friend Dr. Jason Dean very quickly grow a following of people that needed his information. A year ago, many people did not care about his viewpoints. Now, it is a calming influence on people who really need it.

The more over the target Dr. Dean was, the harder the push down from the tech overlords came. He quickly disappeared from Facebook, Twitter, and had his YouTube channel removed.

Rather than let his voice be silenced, he decided to build his own platform and get his message out in other places.

I had agreed with him on many things, not everything, but many things.

It made me question a lot of what I was doing. I had been working on this book manuscript for over a year. The world had changed so much, and I just didn't really feel like the viewpoints I was writing down were mine. I asked myself: "What am I really risking for what I believe in?" The experience of the past year had pushed me, but Dr. Dean gave me the courage.

Then, I asked myself: "What do I really believe?" I actually even had a conversation with my good friend David Brier on the same topic. He led me through an exercise and what follows is what came out of it.

- I'm for a world where participation trophies don't exist; there are winners and losers in life. Self-esteem isn't a right; it's earned by achievement.

- I'm not for Freudian psycho-babel. I'm for empowerment and telling you that something can be done about your struggles.

- I'm for everyone being respected as a human being—hate doesn't look good on you.

- I'm for rewarding people whose statistics are up, not down; whatever you reward more, you'll get more of. To that extent, I believe you keep more of what you earn because you earned it.

- I'm for a world where no one is told their business is "non-essential."

- I'm against telling our children they need drugs because they can't sit still. Rather, I'm for finding out how to teach them better and play to their strengths.

- I'm against recreational drugs; getting dumber doesn't sound like my idea of a good time.

- I believe that adversity is our greatest teacher. Sure, there's 1% of the world that has always been wealthy. However, there are many, which I have interviewed, that came from literally nothing or had it all taken away and achieved at a higher level. The lie is that it's what you're born with; the truth is that you have to be willing to go get it.

- I'm about freedom of thought, religion, the press, movement, and assembly. I may not agree with you, but I'll fight like hell for your right to say it.

- I'm about better conversations that matter. Otherwise, what's the point?

Knowing what I was actually for made me realize that a lot of what I was doing did align with my viewpoints; however, in some areas, I was sacrificing my beliefs. Knowing that, I started to do some interviews that I would not have done before. I interviewed former Overstock.com founder Patrick Byrne because I really wanted to know what people were talking about with voter fraud. Was it real? Was it a lie? I started diving in a substantially deeper topics. I have never had the goal, and still do not have the goal, of being political, but I do want the data to be able to make my own decisions.

In April of this past year, I interviewed mypillow.com founder Mike Lindell. Most of the conversation focused on Mike's incredible story: how he'd come from being a drug addict to founding one of the largest privately held companies in the country, making jobs for thousands of Americans. At the time, Mike was launching a social media platform as well as being one of the loudest voices on voter fraud.

I got a lot of great feedback from the conversation, but something odd, which I did not expect, happened after that. My audience numbers dropped substantially. I even had a former guest call me hateful names I'll not repeat here. I didn't initially think this would be a problem. I didn't take into account others viewpoints. Rather, I was just exploring things I thought were important. I still tried hard not to directly espouse a political view but explore the tough subjects.

However, in a fractured political world, just exploring some topics, right or wrong, was seen as espousing a political point of view.

I know my own heart, and I know God knows my heart. Rather than be discouraged by his words, I was emboldened by them. I was no longer being passive; I was actually making an impact in the subjects people are talking about.

## Extraordinary Story

**George Bryant:** "Why Building Real Relationships is the Key to Building a Billion Dollar Business"

George Bryant is an incredible human being. He served his country in Afghanistan, almost losing his legs. Rather than become bitter, he channeled that pain to help others, leadinging to a brand that helped others to take control of their nutrition and a *NY Times* best seller. He used that experience to help several brands become unicorns through unique customer journeys.

*www.jeremyryanslate.com/bryant*

In my own way, I have found the courage to be extraordinary—to myself, the greatest version of myself, and not sacrifice my own personal beliefs and ethics.

Many times, to be seen in the public eye, I think we're either silent or sacrifice our own ethics because we want to be light. I realized that in doing that, I was not furthering conversations that could help heal the country and bring people together and create a greater impact.

In that experience of truly putting myself out there, in that moment, I found my voice and I started to find my tribe.

I realized that having conversations on difficult topics with people who are well known was a way I could make a huge impact. Over the past six months, it's led me to having conversations on authoritarianism, love, family, the Chinese Communist Party, and the things that affect us each and every day, rather than just presenting a rosy and sunny picture of the world. I strive to understand so that I can make an educated decision. The world can be a scary place, but if you're aware and someone shows you that something can be done about it, you can be so much more causative.

In the first version of my podcast, much was based on self-fulfillment, finding your passion, and bringing online marketing into your life. I think those things are important, but much like the sophomore album from a band, I was exploring the bigger, wider issues and what they meant to me. It makes me think of one of my favorite bands, Brand New. Their first album, entitled *Your Favourite Weapon*, released in 2001, was pop punk; it fit the stream of consciousness of the time, but their second, released in 2003, entitled *Deja Entendu*, was vastly different and became entirely more successful.

Now, when I talk about difficult subjects, I always want to leave people feeling like something can be done about it, but in order to make an impact in the world, you have to really understand the world around you.

I tell you the story of my past year, not to convince you to agree with me, not to change your mind on anything. Rather, it is to show you that even if you're performing at your best, without courage you cannot reach your full potential to be extraordinary and make the impact you seek to make.

## What Does it Mean to be Extraordinary?

If you ask the best in the world what the single greatest secret to success is, they'll sit back in their chair and put their feet up on the desk. They'll take a long, thoughtful pause, and with their hands folded behind the crown of their head, they may start to gently chuckle to themselves.

You're asking the wrong question.

Being extraordinary is not a single element. It cannot be distilled down to one thing. However, we're told that being a success is a magical thing that happens and a place that we'll arrive. The hard part is that this long-held truth is the biggest lie.

### Extraordinary Story

**David Brier:** "Why Entrepreneurs Need Courage"

The greatest single thing an entrepreneur needs is courage. In this short interview, David Brier puts into perspective how you can, no matter your walk of life, make that a reality.

*www.jeremyryanslate.com/bonus-entrepreneurs-need-courage-david-brier*

The fact is that the path that so many follow, the one society sells us on, will not lead to the promised land. The truth is, the route we're all told to take may actually stick us in purgatory, without Dante or Virgil to guide us.

Mark Twain stated: *"Most men die at 27, we just bury them at 72."* It's sad, but if you look at it this closely, you'll realize we're all born with passion, goals, and big dreams, but over time, stumbling aimlessly through life without a clear path beats those things out of us.

Becoming extraordinary takes time and work, but when you know its tenets, it is a repeatable and predictable process.

Over the course of the last six years, I've had conversations with some of the highest performers in the world: Indy 500 winners, *New York Times* bestselling authors, platinum recording artists, billionaires, even the former director of the CIA.

Though their paths and their walks of life are different, they have one thing in common: they are extraordinary. Upon deeper examination, each applied the same principles to achieve the greatness of their life and impact.

They have courage.

They saw adversity as a tool for growth.

They didn't wait to find their passion.

They sought the biggest, scariest goals possible.

They did not allow others to define their success.

They knew they had to be the one to tell their story.

They were radically responsible for their own success.

Being extraordinary is a decision.

The door to being extraordinary is open. Will you walk in?

## My Goal for You, the Reader

The goal for this book is not for it to be another "rah, rah," feel-good story. Rather, it will delve into the stories of some people I've interviewed, some I haven't, and others I've really admired.

It will be a mix of storytelling, experiences from my own life and study, as well as those from wider culture, where you learn about these individuals lives, their experiences and the things that made them great. Each chapter will leave you with something at the end that you can implement into your life so that you, too, can create the greatest version of yourself. That extraordinary part of yourself.

This is not personal development in the traditional sense of personal development. If I had to compare it to anything, it's more like *Plutarch's Lives*, a compilation of stories of great people, who, at the time, were either still living or had lived and died and accomplished great things. The Roman scholar Plutarch, who lived during the first and second century AD, arranged these biographies so that the lessons of these men's lives could be learned from.

No one is born extraordinary, but they become so based on how they live their lives and the lessons they learn from them. You, too, can embrace that viewpoint and become extraordinary.

## JJ Virgin

JJ Virgin is one of the most famous names in the fitness industry. She has a globally recognized brand and is a *New York Times* bestselling author. When JJ earned her title as a bestselling author, she was going through one of the most difficult periods of her life.

JJ nearly lost her son to an accident nearly weeks before her book, *The Virgin Diet*, would launch. She knew that only the success of the book could save him.

She took courage in the fact that she needed to succeed; she had no other option. Sometimes in life, we can succeed when we are really afraid because we are working for something bigger than ourselves. For JJ, that was the life of her son.

## Courage in Spite of Insurmountable Odds

When JJ got a book deal for *The Virgin Diet*, she decided she wanted a half-a-million- dollar book advance because her co-star on *Freaky Eaters* had gotten the same sum. Dollar advance. JJ had been on *Dr. Phil* for two years and done many things that her co-star hadn't. She decided that if he could do it, she could do it.

She compares it to running a four-minute mile; once you break that barrier, it's easier to go even further. Her agent went and got her a $520,000 book deal. She wasn't quite sure how her agent pulled it off, since she had a failed book and her reality show had just gotten canceled. She was excited, but she viewed all the money that she brought in as money to market the book.

She invested all the money in the book and she also borrowed money for the book. She had a great idea that she would run a public television show to help support the book launch. She was only weeks out from that launch when everything changed for her.

JJ's son was crossing the street and was hit and run by a driver and left for dead. When she first arrived at the hospital, the doctor informed her that he was going to die. The nature of his injuries were so severe, he was not going to make it through the night.

The doctors believed that he would never survive the airlift, but in order for him to have a chance at life it needed to happen. However, the doctor believed even if he survived the airlift, it wouldn't be worth it. Her 15-year-old son then asked the doctor if his brother's survival rate would be about 25%. The doctor agreed. Her son then stated, "It's not zero, Mom. We'll take those odds." So they overruled the doctor and her son made it through the airlift. When he got to the hospital, he went immediately into surgery. JJ's son had 13 fractures and had just gotten rods put into his femurs.

He was on life support, he was in a coma, and JJ just looked at him and said aloud, "Grant, you're going to be 110%." She knew she would have to go with the biggest most outlandish thing, meaning not just 100% but 110%. Though he was in a coma, she was very confident he could hear her. She repeated herself, "You're going to be 110%."

JJ had decided that she had to fight. She was going to pool her resources; she was going to do whatever she had to do in order to help her son. What that actually meant is her book had to go to bestseller, because she was so invested at this point that if she didn't do so, she would be bankrupt. If she were bankrupt, she would not be able to help her son.

She had to get going on the book. It was coming out in just a matter of weeks. When she looks back, she realizes she published a *New York Times* bestseller sitting next to her son, who is in a coma, while she was on her laptop. She knew she was not going to leave her son's side, but she also knew that her book had to be a success. Coming back and forth from the hospital was a two-hour journey, time she was not willing to take away from her son.

## 🎤 Extraordinary Story

**Duff Gibson:** "The Oldest Winter Olympics Gold Medalist and the Tao of Sport"

Duff Gibson knew he wanted to be an Olympian, to the point that he tried several sports to do it before settling on the skeleton. Duff then went on to win a gold medal at 39, making him the oldest winter Olympics gold medalist.

*www.jeremyryanslate.com/gibson*

JJ remembers that when you get to that point, it really feels like do or die. In that place when you make a decision and there's only one way it can go. It puts your back up against the wall and puts you in a position that you must win. She had to put her health first, because she could not be sick because then she could not see her son in the ICU. He had holes in his brain and could not be exposed to infection. She could not go in there with illness. She knew if she was going to get her son to 110%, then she herself needed to be 110%. It gave her a new viewpoint on self-care, and that's when she knew she was going to blow the book up. She cut everything out of her life that didn't need to be there and just looked at the essentials.

## Automate, Delegate, Delete

It was in that moment that JJ learned a lesson she took with her the rest of her life. She took this extreme negative and turned it into something that she's able to use every time she releases a new project. She calls it automate, delegate, delete. She does these things on a daily basis, figuring out where time is wasted. Those things that don't matter. She cut out all social media before noon unless it makes money. Those things that are a waste of time. When referencing social media, JJ says:

> "You're just like, where did that time go? Why is my thumb sore? And where did that time go? And, and all it's made you do is feel bad about yourself because you've looked at everybody else and their life.
>
> Seeing that this picture I have was Seth Godin's now all over the place. And so everyone's like, well, JJ is out there hanging out with Seth Goden and all these people every single day, when they don't realize, that was one day out of 365 days."

The rest of the time she's normal just like everyone else. She thinks that social media is one of those things that can be delegated and sometimes deleted out of our lives. In that conversation of social media, JJ gets back to the content creation she was using to drive her book. "It's something I think most people are familiar with. You're wearing that perfect shirt, your hair is done, but you're wearing sweatpants. Video only sees the top half of our body, so we are always aware of what's on camera."

At that point in time, she was in the middle of a move; she was sitting in a temporary condo, waiting for her house to close. All this while her son was in the hospital. She turned the corner of the master bedroom into a makeup studio and set up a desk, lights, and a camera, and that's where she filmed the content to promote her book.

She laughs when people think of the glamorous lives people see from the outside realizing that so many of us as entrepreneurs, as extraordinary people, are really just trying to make it go right. Some are doing so on bigger scales and bigger stages than others.

That push on only concentrating on her own health, the health of her son, and things that led to her book being a success, led *The Virgin Diet* to being a massive success and saw it spend 26 weeks on a *New York Times* bestseller list and change millions of lives.

For JJ, success was not optional. It's why she's tried to create the same mindset for herself when she's on a big project: automate, delegate, delete. Not from the viewpoint of her children's safety, but from the viewpoint of realizing the things that get in the way of you producing the things you want and creating the results you want. That viewpoint, and that event in her life have changed her trajectory drastically.

Now, years down the road, her son is doing well, she's one of the most recognized names in the health and fitness space, and she's a well-known *New York Times* bestselling author. The terrible experience of her son's accident taught her the process of automating, delegating, and deleting. One of the biggest lessons that she brings into every part of her life. It's also shown her what she is willing to do to be successful.

JJ is willing to walk through walls for success. When people compliment her on her success, she finds herself wondering, *Are they willing to do what I've done to get here? Are they willing to work seven days a week and miss that party? Are they willing to not go on any vacations and do all the things I've been doing to be successful as an entrepreneur?* She realizes success doesn't come overnight, and she realizes the amount of effort she's had to put in to succeed.

## Extraordinary Takeaway

The *American Heritage Dictionary* defines courage as: *The state or quality of mind or spirit that enables one to face danger, fear, or vicissitudes with self-possession, confidence, and resolution; bravery.*

Bravery means not operating from a place of fear. So, from here on out, you are no longer operating from a place of fear. Rather, you are now operating from a place of bravery and courage.

Up to this point in your life, you may not have been courageous. This is, in fact, the perfect time to start. I don't know who said it, but it's been said that *"the best time to plant a tree is 50 years ago; the next best time is right now."* This does not mean that you need to lead an army into battle, or stop an armed robber. For you, this may be something simple. Courage itself is something that people look at from different perspectives. What may be courageous for me, you may not see as courageous.

Maybe you take courage for others in your life as JJ Virgin did for her son. She knew that failure could not be an option for her because only if she was successful could she pay for her son's medical care. It takes courage to look at the odds and decide you will make it happen in spite of them.

It is, however, a gradient scale. You define what is courageous is for you. No one else can do that for you You can do one more courageous thing today than you did yesterday. And that's how, from this point forward, you should look at every day of your life. *"How can I be stronger and more courageous than I was yesterday?" "How can I be true to myself, not someone else's opinion of me?"* Each day, you should be trying to be better than the day before.

Moving forward, start by making the decision to be courageous. It took me 32 years to make that decision. One in which I realized my personal integrity mattered to me more than what others thought. I was willing to speak about, in a thoughtful way, subjects I would have avoided before. Living in my truth took realizing some people would change their opinion of me and wouldn't like me, but I had to be able to look myself in the mirror at night.

Whatever age you are in life, now is the perfect time to start. Courage for me was more about speaking my mind and not speaking to please others. For you, it may be starting with a schedule so that you can reach a goal. Whatever that brave decision is that a person of courage would make, now that you are a person of courage, make that decision.

I'm pulling for you.

# 2. Your Mo Lewis Moment

*Nothing in the world is worth having or worth doing unless it means effort, pain, difficulty... I have never in my life envied a human being who led an easy life. I have envied a great many people who led difficult lives and led them well.*

—Theodore Roosevelt

Adversity is the greatest test of a person. In fact, the original thought of this book was to write only of adversity, but a person is made up of more than that. Merriam-Webster defines adversity as "a state or instance of serious or continued difficulty or misfortune." Honestly, that is putting it lightly.

There is no quality of it; there is no quantity of it. The only evidence that it exists is for one to live it. It is the crucible; it is the blacksmith's furnace. What I mean by that is that it is that thing that allows for transformation. It helps someone to become who they were meant to be.

Historically, if you look at many impactful individuals, their trajectory in life was either changed or honed by what they had to overcome. Adversity in itself is a process of transformation. It is not a single moment; rather, it is a metamorphosis. Adversity is the caterpillar that cocoons itself, hidden from the world and slowly becoming its higher-level self.

Adversity is that thing that is in the eye of the beholder. What is a great adversity for me may not be a great adversity for you and vice versa. It's something very personal. The choices we make can increase or lessen it. The point in our life at which we encounter it and the people around us can change how we experience and perceive it.

Sometimes, great athletes get to a level where they need to create it; others continually experience it. During the 1998 finals, the Bulls were highly favored against the Utah Jazz, but teams at that level still need to motivate themselves.

## 🎙 Extraordinary Story

**Mark Eaton**: "NBA All-Star & Record Holder's 4 Commitments to a Winning Team"

Mark Eaton is a two-time, NBA Defensive Player of the Year, as well as the single season record holder in blocks. Mark played for legendary Utah Jazz teams, alongside John Stockton and Karl Malone. In the 1990s, the Utah Jazz played Michael Jordan's Chicago Bulls in the NBA Finals on multiple occasions. He has a unique perspective on not just being at the top of his field, but also competing against one of the best athletes ever to play.

*www.jeremyryanslate.com/eaton*

Michael Jordan was eating dinner when one of the Jazz coaches walked into the restaurant. Noticing him, Jordan waved him over, but the coach didn't acknowledge him. Michael was shocked. They had both worked together with Dean Smith at North Carolina; it was a huge slight that this coach disrespected him. Jordan decided that because of this, he was not just going to beat the Jazz...he was going to dominate them.

The more likely explanation here is that in a crowded restaurant, the coach just didn't see Jordan; no slight, no ill will. However, as someone that is extraordinary, Michael Jordan had to create the motivation to win. That series led Jordan's Bulls to win the championship, his sixth and final as a player.

Adversity is that thing that teaches us to keep going. As Abraham Lincoln stated: *"I will prepare and some day my chance will come."* Adversity is the lock, and preparation is the key. Adversity makes us the person we need to be in order to overcome; it creates that hardiness we need to have.

We always need to be preparing for our moment to come. In life, success is when preparation meets the correct circumstances. For Ray Kroc, it was in his 50s. For Colonel Harland Sanders, it was much later in life. For Tom Brady, it was in his second year playing in the NFL.

To me, the story of Tom Brady is the greatest example of preparation meeting circumstances. Had it not been for a single moment, Tom Brady might have been a career backup. That moment is what I like to call the *"Mo Lewis moment,"* a moment when the preparation that we have spent our entire lives on meets the circumstances. The name comes from the former Jets linebacker that hit then Patriots quarterback Drew Bledsoe, knocking him out of the game and bringing Tom Brady into the game.

We all have those moments. Some of us aren't ready. Others cannot recognize those moments when they occur. So, not only is it about preparation; it is being able to recognize an opportunity in the adversity presented in front of you.

Tom Brady is arguably the best quarterback ever to play in the National Football League. Whether you're a Patriots fan (or later in his career, a Buccaneers fan) or not, you have to just appreciate what Tom Brady has done as a player.

As of this writing, here are the records that Brady Holds:

- Seven-time Super Bowl champion (XXXVI, XXXVIII, XXXIX, XLIX, LI, LIII, LV)
- Six-time Super Bowl MVP (XXXVI, XXXVIII, XLIX, LI, LV)
- Three-time NFL Most Valuable Player (2007, 2010, 2017)
- Fifteen-time Pro Bowl (2001, 2004, 2005, 2007, 2009–2018, 2021)
- Three-time First-team All-Pro (2007, 2010, 2017)
- Three-time Second-team All-Pro (2005, 2016, 2021)
- Two-time NFL Offensive Player of the Year (2007, 2010)
- Five-time NFL passing touchdowns leader (2002, 2007, 2010, 2015, 2021)
- Four-time NFL passing yards leader (2005, 2007, 2017, 2021)
- Two-time NFL passer rating leader (2007, 2010)
- NFL completion percentage leader (2007)
- *Sporting News* NFL Athlete of the Decade (2010s)
- Associated Press Male Athlete of the Year (2007)
- *Sports Illustrated* Sportsman of the Year (2005)
- NFL 2000s All-Decade Team
- NFL 100th Anniversary All-Time Team

The story about Brady had always been about how he had a chip on his shoulder because he was drafted in the sixth round (out of seven, 199th overall) out of seven rounds in the NFL Draft. However, until reading *Brady vs Manning* by Gary Meyers,[1] I didn't fully understand how the chip on Brady's shoulder was created.

---

1. Meyers, Gary, *Brady vs Manning: The Untold Story of the Rivalry That Transformed the NFL*, New York, NY Crown Publishing Group, 2017

It was about so much more than being a sixth-round pick. Tom Brady attended the renowned Junipero Serra High School in San Mateo, California. The school was also attended by such sports legends as Barry Bonds and Lynn Swann.

As a sophomore, Brady didn't start on a JV squad that was 0-8; he started on the varsity team, only because the starter got hurt. He would not relinquish that role until graduation, finishing all-state as well as winning his team's MVP award.

Heading into college, Brady was a highly sought-after prospect and decided upon Michigan since he was assured of a starting spot early on. He redshirted his freshman year. Michigan had a full quarterback room, so he would still have four more years of eligibility.

The coach and athletic director that recruited Brady abruptly left and changed the entire setting for Brady. He was buried at seventh on the depth chart behind future NFL player, Brian Griese, who led Michigan to a national championship in 1997.

## Extraordinary Fact

Tom Brady's achievements as a quarterback are impressive, and it's equally impressive that he really ever made it into the league based on his story. Here, I want to point out just how hard it is to make it in the NFL.

I read a 2021 study by Sports Skeeda about NCAA Football players and going pro that really puts it in perspective.[2] There are 1,093,234 high school football players in America. Of those players, 6.5%, or 71,060

2. Cesconetto, Giovani Izidorio, *How many NCAA football players make it to the NFL?*, 2021, https://www.sportskeeda.com/college-football/how-many-ncaa-football-players-make-nfl

will ever play in college. Of that number, only 1.6% will ever play professional football.

The above facts truly put into perspective how important concentrating on your craft, like Tom Brady, is if you want to go pro.

There's also more to this equation. As of this writing, Tom Brady is 45 years old, leading the league in passing touchdowns. Tom is on a very short list of players that have played above the age of 40,[3] not many of them playing at the level at which he is. His longevity and ability to compete past 40 is extraordinary.

According to Statistica,[4] the average span of an NFL career is 3.3 years. Running backs have the shortest average career at 2.57 years, and kickers have the longest average career at 4.87 years. Quarterbacks, like Brady, who is in his 23rd season at the time of this writing, average 4.44 years.

Not only is it extraordinary that Brady made it into the league and started but also that he is still playing more than five times the average career for a quarterback.

Brady sat behind Griese for two years before finally getting a chance to start his junior year. However, his position was never solid, as he was competing with New York Yankees' prospect Drew Hensen for playing time.

At this, author Gary Meyers remarked, "How could they sit Tom Brady?" Well, he wasn't Tom Brady yet.

---

3. Pro Football Hall of Fame Editor, *40 and Over Club*, 2021, https://www.profootballhof.com/football-history/40-and-over-club/
4. Gough, Christina, *Average playing career length in the National Football League*, 2019, https://www.statista.com/statistics/240102/average-player-career-length-in-the-national-football-league/

Brady's senior season he was platooned with Hensen for the first seven games before getting the reins for the remaining schedule.

As a pro prospect, Brady wasn't the most athletic, didn't have the biggest arm, and due to his competition with Hensen, wasn't seen as a future star. The Patriots coach Bill Belichick took a chance on Brady in the sixth round.

Brady spent his first season with the Patriots as the fourth quarterback; NFL teams rarely have that many on the active roster. In his second season, he climbed to backing up the Patriots' hundred-million-dollar quarterback, Drew Bledsoe.

In the second game of the 2001 season, Bledsoe was tackled by Jets linebacker Mo Lewis. Bledsoe left the game with a life-threatening injury, and Brady became the starter. Brady led the Patriots to a Super Bowl championship that season, in addition to five more as the Patriots quarterback.

The seven Super Bowl wins as a quarterback is the most any quarterback has ever achieved. The next closest is a tie between Terry Bradshaw and Joe Montana at four.

## Extraordinary Story

**Brian Dawkins**: "Humility, Commitment and What Separates Average from the Hall of Fame"

Brian Dawkins played nearly his entire career with the Philadelphia Eagles of the NFL. He came into the league as an undersized player that had a lot of average ability. What Brian also had was incredible work ethic and drive to be the best. He built a Hall of Fame career by being willing to work longer and harder by any player that he was put next to.

*www.jeremyryanslate.com/dawkins*

The greatest gift you can receive is being an underdog—having a "chip on your shoulder." Being an underdog is actually a leg up. It gives you something to drive for and push for—the opportunity to prove wrong those who thought you didn't have a right to be there. Underdogs know they have to work harder. They know that life was not just given to them.

Had Tom Brady had it easy, been a four-year starter and the first overall pick, there's a good chance he would not have led his team to seven Super Bowl Championships.

Because he was never the best, Brady never just relied on talent; he always needed the edge. That led to him creating his own workout routine to transform his body, watching more hours of film, and even bringing players to his home to train.

To become the greatest quarterback ever to play in the NFL, Tom Brady needed to transform, but he also needed to learn to deal with disappointment. He needed to be taught the hard way why you keep showing up and what real leadership looks like.

That's why those who have it all given to them rarely reach the pinnacle. The adversity that people go through helps them to build not just the person they need to be but also the routines that they need to become extraordinary.

Routines are what people that are extraordinary work on without fail. They are that preparation that we have for when our day comes. Being extraordinary is about always preparing for that Mo Lewis moment when it's presented in front of you.

Though I'll discuss it later in this book, in my conversation with Former CIA Director and Four-Star General, David Petraeus, I learned more of the same around this concept of luck meeting preparation. Petraeus stated:

*"Hard work can, can improve your chances of success. That focus, that trying to be again, obviously the best you can be, that life is a competitive endeavor, embrace it.*

*You don't get a t-shirt just for showing up in the real world; you have to. Success can enable future opportunities. I really did believe, from a very early time in uniform, that luck is what happens when preparation meets opportunity. I was determined to be as prepared as I could be. If there was a call for that preparation at some time, it is fair for people to look at my career and say, 'Well, gosh, you know, Petraeus has got lucky here or there.'*

*There is truth in that. There's a number of times, along in my career, where something happened. That was just timing. Luck would have you, but you have to keep showing up and working hard in order to get lucky. Right? Sometimes, as well, I've said, luck is what happens when preparation meets opportunity.*

*And so if the opportunity presents itself, can you capitalize, can you make the most?"*

Therefore, prepare, and your time will come. You never can predict when that will be; be vigilant.

## Raising Our Ability to Take It

We all have a natural state that our bodies rest at. The human body at homeostasis is always at an average of 98.6 degrees. One could look at adversity as a way to reset that thermometer.

Why do the Green Bay Packers always play better on their home field when it's snowing and close to zero degrees Fahrenheit?

They have embraced the cold; they can function at a level colder than your average player. In fact, some crazy Packers players, like

Aaron Jones, can be seen on a January day wearing short sleeves. Their thermometer is set to function at more extreme conditions.

## 🎤 Extraordinary Story

**Anthony Trucks**: "How this Former NFL Pro Turned Adversity to a Shift to Purpose"

Anthony is one of the single biggest stories of adversity I have ever heard. From everything he has been through, he should be bitter, but he has more love for humanity than any person I have ever met. He lived in the foster system for a while before really having a family. He was a stand-out football player at the University of Oregon and went undrafted to the NFL before a shoulder injury ended his career. Then, Anthony started a gym, but his marriage fell apart and he later lost the gym. He started working on himself, put his marriage back together, and is now creating the career of his dreams. Anthony Trucks knows how to channel adversity.

*www.jeremyryanslate.com/trucks*

What about when someone who has dealt with a Florida summer comes to a New Jersey in the summer? They're so used to the heat and humidity, that 80 degrees Fahrenheit in New Jersey makes them reach for a North Face. They can deal with heat and humidity better.

That same concept can be applied to adversity. If you have had to deal with not knowing what you're going to eat, you can take more. If you have had to clean urine off the bathroom floor, you can take more.

When you've worked two jobs and put in a seventeen-hour day, you can work longer and harder. When you've overcome a traumatic experience, you can take more psychological and emotional stress.

Your thermometer is set to a higher temperature than others. When others bristle at a little discomfort, you chuckle, see your advantage, and go for what you want.

For Tom Brady, the best example of this is two specific seasons; the 2016-17 and 2020-21 seasons.

In the 2017 Super Bowl, Brady's Patriots seemed all but beaten. With only 8.31 seconds left in the third quarter, Brady's Patriots trailed the offensive juggernaut that was the Atlanta Falcons 28-3. It seemed as though the game was over and the Patriots dynasty was coming to a close.

Then the veteran quarterback led his team on a 13-play, 75-yard touchdown drive that included a fourth-down conversion to wide receiver Danny Amendola. The Patriots missed an extra point but inched back to 28-9. With ten minutes left, Brady led his team down the field for a field goal. The score was now 28-12.

Next, the defense came to support Brady. Falcons quarterback Matt Ryan was sacked and fumbled the ball on the 25-yard line. Brady led the team in for the short score, followed by the two-point conversion; 28-20 with five minutes remaining. With only minutes remaining, and starting on their own 9-yard line, Brady led the team down the field for another score and a two-point conversion; the game went to overtime, tied at 28.

The Patriots started overtime with the ball and promptly marched down the field and scored to end the game. Brady was, again, a Super Bowl Champion.

Brady was able to deliver when Falcons quarterback Matt Ryan could not. It's a simple application of the adversity thermometer. Ryan was a first-round pick that did not have to struggle like Brady did to get there; his thermometer was not set as high. Therefore, with the game on the line, in a high-pressure situation, Brady came through. He had been through so much that he was calm, cool, and collected when it mattered; adversity had prepared him for the greatest comeback in Super Bowl history.

In the 2020-21 season, it was a world that no one was prepared for. A pandemic shut down the world. It seemed as if there would be no sports, and when they finally resumed, there was no real off season, no pre-season games, and players were at a very distinct disadvantage if they were with a new team. After 20 years as a member of the New England Patriots, the team moved on from the 43-year-old quarterback, believing that his best years were behind him.

The season was a greater hardship than can be expected for any player to compete in, but if you are someone like Brady, who has a high thermometer for adversity, it wasn't.

Tom Brady signed with the Tampa Bay Buccaneers. Not only was the season preparation not there, but players were also obligated to a number of restrictions to fight the COVID-19 pandemic, including testing and quarantines. Most teams played in front of empty stadiums, for fear of the virus spreading.

Five weeks in, the Bucs were 3-2 and there was talk of Brady's age catching up with him. In addition, a media-created soap opera played out about disputes between Brady and coach Bruce Arians.

By week 13, the Bucs were 7-5 and a lot had to go right for them to make the playoffs, much less win a Super Bowl. The team went on to win eight straight games, including a demolition of the favored Kansas City Chiefs in the Super Bowl, 31-9. Cool under pressure, Brady had his seventh Super Bowl and his fifth Super Bowl MVP.

Set your thermometer high, and you, too, can be cool under pressure.

## Extraordinary Takeaway

You must understand that there will always be adversity in your life. You cannot control adversity; it will happen. You cannot control opportunity; it will happen.

Though I've never been a Boy Scout, the goal is for the Boy Scout motto, *"always be prepared,"* to become your new motto. You need to be prepared for every eventuality when that moment comes. The days may be harder, the days may be easier, but you need to show up as the best version of yourself every single day. It is actually in consistency that greatness finds a place to grow.

Nothing in life is given, and thus it shouldn't be taken for granted. When an opportunity comes, you can't say, *"I wasn't ready."* You need to always be ready for the day that opportunity presents itself, because it will. If you're not ready, you'll just be another person talking about what might have been.

You also may currently believe that this moment has already came and went for you. Don't let thoughts like these discourage you. We get many opportunities in life to make things happen. Do we often miss one because we weren't prepared? Yes, we do, but there is still always a chance to prepare for that next one.

Remember, opportunities come to those who can actually see them. While some see opportunities, others see nothing. So, not only do you need to be prepared, but you also need to be one who can see the opportunities for when they actually come so that you take full advantage of them.

Moving on from here, you're a Boy Scout. *"Always be prepared."*

# 3. Don't Follow Your Passion

*Follow your passion is easily the worst
advice you could ever give or get.*

— Mark Cuban

There's an epidemic right now. And it's not the type you're thinking about. It's not a disease; it's something more horrible.

This epidemic is an idea, and it's widespread. It's this idea people have that the world will come to them. They're waiting for the skies to open and their purpose to emerge in front of them. They're waiting for someone to pay them $15 an hour to do something that a machine at a Taco Bell can do.

They're looking for that participation trophy; that person to recognize them and tell them they're special and important; that there's something unique and better about them than everyone else.

Extraordinary people know that life isn't like that. They know that life is about finding something you're good at and continually working at that thing and working at that thing and working at that thing until it becomes effortless. Passion comes after putting in the hard work. It does not come before.

This was something I reflected on quite a bit this year, as at sixty-seven, my dad has been getting ready to retire. My dad is the single hardest working individual I've ever met. In his late teens and early twenties, it looked like he had a trajectory to play professional baseball.

He had all the skills: a hard moving fastball, a curveball that dropped three feet, the ability to hit a ball a long way, and the skill to play the outfield like a pitcher should just not be able to. The stereotypical player like Mickey Mantle or Mike Trout is called a five-tool player; they have all the tools you would want for an incredible baseball player; my dad had six tools—he could also pitch.

When that didn't pan out for him, he started working for a company called the Ames Rubber Corporation in the machine shop. It was one of the lowest level positions that you could take, but it was a door to be able to create something of himself. My dad worked hard every single day of his life and took every single opportunity he could to improve himself or to improve his position at the company.

Over the years, that hard work paid off in spades, leading him to being one of the top managerial positions of the company. In 2001, he decided he needed a new game.

He started working for a company much further away, Star Glo Industries, but in this company, he became their director of quality. The incredible part about it is that before him, they did not have a quality control department. He built and created every single process the company had. He even helped them to become ISO compliant, one of the hardest certifications to get.

He was a self-made man, proving the American Dream is real. For me, he has been the greatest influence in my life in working hard, getting good, and finding the no-effort zone.

The no-effort zone is the highest level of skill. Your work has become part of you. This is where something has become second nature and you're just so darn good at it. That doesn't mean that you're not actually putting effort in, but that it takes less hard work to actually get something done.

That is the area where true passion is found. It doesn't come down from the skies to find you. You find it. It's an active process, not a passive process. You find your passion through doing and working, not through waiting.

This thought epidemic isn't just a failure of culture but of education. Our education system is based on the humanistic school of the 1700s. The school is not based on helping people become entrepreneurs or helping people to create jobs. Rather, this system of education was developed for training people for what was, at the time, a budding Industrial Revolution. Now, as we stand on the precipice of a Technological Revolution, current schooling and training is no longer set up in a way that will help people get results in creating the lives they want to create.

Therefore, we are disadvantaged not just by the way we're educated rows of the dreams we are sold. I say disadvantaged because traditional education does not put emphasis on application and secondly because we're sold all these great things education will get us and its not true.

Most personal development espouses this rosy outlook about the world: *"Decide what you want and you'll get it"* or *"Do something you love and never work a day in your life."*

There are even influencers like Gary Vaynerchuk saying, *"Don't do things you hate."* However, to be successful in life you're going to have to do a lot of things you don't like to do. That's just how it works. The missing element in this statement is working experience. In my life, I found that, but I've also seen that in the hundreds of people I've interviewed, a lot of them started at a low level; started out disadvantaged and worked their way to where they are.

They were willing to outwork those that would not work. I guess the old adage "hard work beats talent when talent doesn't work hard" is very true in many cases.

First, let's return to the topic of education. Then, I want to talk about a method that really works for how you can really create a career for yourself in the future.

## The Education Problem

I want to start at the point where we're all led astray, and for most of us, it is for a lot of our lives. I've often said I'm way too educated for my own good; I have a master's degree. I studied in Europe. I did all that kind of extravagant stuff. And I don't use any of that education. Well, more accurately, it's not that I don't use it; through my education, I've honed my ability to research anything. However, my career really has nothing to do with what I went to school for.

For many of the extraordinary individuals I've spoken to, that rings the same. Helio Castroneves didn't go to school to be a race car driver; he just did it. Grant Cardone went to school to be an accountant but worked hard to make himself into the ultimate salesperson. Kara Goldin built the Hint Water company from the ground up, not from taking a course on how to do it.

Life experience and hard work can be some of the best teachers.

I think, overall, that are education system is broken, and we need to look at some ways we can fix it. Our education system wasn't made to build future entrepreneurs and leaders.

This is becoming an increasingly difficult issue to even discuss. Apparently, education is a social issue. Earlier this year on Facebook, when talking about an interview I had done on education, Facebook marked it as fake news! It was odd to me—the warning also said that this was a social issue when I tried to run advertising on the post but couldn't. I thought to myself: Social issues seem to be the things we all care about, so why am I not allowed to run advertising on this?

In my discussion with philosopher James Lindsay, issues with public discussion of education policy really started with the government underwriting of student loans and colleges trying to please their customers.

Even though it's becoming a murkier topic to discuss, I believe it is an issue that we have a *responsibility* to talk about. Education is what actually creates the next generation of adults, so any social issues created in college and how it functions will become a future problem if we do not take responsibility for it.

The post I wrote on Facebook, discussing a podcast interview, was important; the topic was college. I think as a society we put too much importance on college. I remember being 17 years old and looking at my first car. My parents were sure to tell me that I would be better off saving my money because college was expensive, and if I wanted to make something of myself, I needed to go. Neither of my parents went to college, though both were very hard-working. Honestly, the thing I learned from them is that hard work is way more valuable than education, especially if it is impractical education.

Knowledge itself really appears to be a poor investment. There are several careers that someone should have to have a college-level education to enter into. For example, I don't want a doctor operating on me if he doesn't have the necessary education or a lawyer representing me if she doesn't know the law inside and out. However, for most careers, life experience is quite important, as opposed to the ability to go to college.

For example, most trades, like plumbers, HVAC techs, and others, are in desperate need of people to do them. In fact, the reason that Mike Rowe created the TV show *Dirty Jobs*, was to create enthusiasm for people going into trades. It was really a public relations campaign to make others aware that jobs that don't need college exist and one can be paid quite well for them.

## Extraordinary Fact

According to a 2018 study by CNBC,[5] neary 40% of college grads take a career after graduation that does not require a degree. In addition, nearly 1 in 5 graduates are still working in a career that does not require a degree ten years after graduation.

It was also found that business majors have a 47% and education majors have a 50% chance of being underemployed, whereas engineering majors only have a 29% chance and computer science majors only have a 30% chance of being underemployed.

Those statistics not only make you consider when and if you need to go to college; they also make you take a second look at the career you are choosing before college.

If you look at the price of college against the price of inflation, the price of college has increased dramatically in the last 100 years. If you ask me, rather than "higher education," college has become High School Part 2 and additionally, it's become a scheme for banks to make money on the everyday person - debt slavery.

What we should look into is helping those that want to start a business. I can remember my first couple years in business. Education is an investment that may or may not pay off, but in my opinion, if we invested in businesses rather than school, it may be a better investment.

---

5. Nova, Amy, *Why your first job out of college really, really matters*, 2018, https://www. cnbc.com/2018/06/25/why-your-first-job-out-of-college-really-really-matters.html

It was almost impossible to get business credit. Then, eventually, after a couple successful years, the bank let me have a $2,500 business credit card. This company had produced hundreds of thousands of dollars in revenue and created many jobs.

On the flipside, if you look at kids starting college at 17 or 18 years old, they're offered hundreds of thousands of dollars in loans for which they have no collateral, and most will never be able to pay back these loans.

It's due to that exorbitant amount of funding than colleges are often spending money on really weird stuff, like an herb garden or some other waste of funding.

Over-education created this new problem. At 22 years old, I graduated with a bachelor's degree and to really distinguish myself, it seemed like I really needed a master's degree. However, upon graduating with a master's degree, I was overqualified for most entry-level jobs and underqualified for most jobs that required a doctorate.

This creates a whole new set of problems. Students graduate college with hundreds of thousands of dollars of debt and no means to ever pay it off. In fact, a very small percentage of people will ever actually get a job in the field that they study for. According to Brad Plumer, 62.1% of college graduates work in a job that doesn't require a degree. Worse yet, only 27.3% had a job that was even related to their major at all.[6]

Even worse, many of the careers that students are going to school for many years for don't actually have salaries that are high enough for the student to pay off all the debt they take on to get those careers.

The problems here is wide-ranging; it creates something very new—debt slavery. Students are graduating college with what amounts to

---

6. Plumer, Brad, *Only 27 percent of college grads have a job related to their major*, 2013, https://www.washingtonpost.com/news/wonk/wp/2013/05/20/only-27-percent-of-college-grads-have-a-job-related-to-their-major/

a mortgage, without actually owning a home. Many of those interest rates are way higher than the standard interest rates for loans. I remember getting my first student loan at a time when my parents were not in a position to co-sign for me. My first student loans were almost 8% interest. Compare that with getting my first mortgage, where my interest rate was under 3%.

So track with me here; students get out of school with a large amount of debt, of which the payments can't even service the interest being taken on daily. So, graduates can't buy a home or buy a car, and they don't have enough money to invest. In order just to make things go, they have to make a lot of money.

Entry-level jobs, especially non-specialized ones, don't pay very much money and continue to worsen the problem, forcing students to rely on credit cards, look for other solutions, such as borrowing money from parents, or default on their student loan payments.

## Extraordinary Story

**Isaac M. Morehouse:** "Redesigning the Education System for Real Results"

Isaac is an intriguing human being who is revolutionizing the education world. Disenchanted by "big education," Isaac created two companies that help to fill the apprenticeships gap and help people get the skills to create the career they want.

*www.jeremyryanslate.com/morehouse*

That problem takes away one of the best parts of entrepreneurship: learning on the job and having it be okay to make mistakes, because you will screw up. There is no room to make mistakes because of the amount of student debt that is due immediately due on graduation. It must be perfect and perfect immediately. New businesses are ugly and rarely perfect, closing the door to most college graduates overcome with debt.

So, we need to either change this system or go on a campaign to help others understand that not everyone needs school to create true prosperity.

Even further, we could look at truly figuring out how to change the payment structure within this system. What if colleges and universities were invested in someone's career after they graduated?

Here's what I mean: the student will pay 15% of total tuition up front. They have to be invested. They have to have some skin in the game. It can't just be free. Free is very easy to quit, and free is very easy not to commit to. Then the university would make a percentage of every year for five years after someone graduates; let's say, 15%.

So, if a university was going to make 15% of your income to help recoup what it cost to educate you for five years after you graduated school, they would be much more motivated to see that your skills actually apply to generating income. This would create two outcomes; number one, education would be perceived as more valuable since schools would have to be more selective, and number two, there would be more emphasis on the ability of the graduate to be a productive member of society.

In this case, there may still be loans since all of us have different economic situations, but they would be substantially lower and would help people to actually create something when they get out of school rather than being drastically hampered.

Anyway, that's my case for changing the system. Now getting back to extraordinary people and how they look at this. Education, at this point in time, when it costs as much as it does, can seem like an anchor around someone's neck when actually, it should be something that helps them further their experience and figure out what they want to do with their life and the value they're going to add to the world.

Extraordinary people fully understand that the value they bring to the world will be the value of the compensation they receive. It may sound a bit Ayn Rand inspired, but its true. It's value given for value received. A good example of this is Adam Curry and John C. Dvorak. Producing the *No Agenda Show* since 2007, they fund the show entirely through listener donations. As long as John and Adam continue to produce a podcast valuable to their listeners, they will continue to donate and the two men continue to be able to do what they love; podcasting.

Curry is known in the podcast world as the "Pod Father," for being the pioneer of podcasting. Which he continues now with his creation of podcasting 2.0, a platform that connects podcasting and blockchain, with podcasters being paid in relation to value received by listeners. Just as he has for a long time, Adam Curry continues to operate from a place of value received being commensurate with value created. So, extraordinary people place a ton emphasis on personal learning. Much of what they do wasn't taught in school and, for many reasons, never will be.

## Extraordinary Fact

- The average person changes jobs 12 times in their lifetime, according to the latest available public survey data (2019).

- The average employee stays with their employer for 4.1 years as of January 2020.

- However, this number varies slightly between women (3.9 years) and men (4.3 years).

- Men hold 12.5 jobs in their lifetime, on average, while women have 12.1 jobs.[7]

So, in order to be more extraordinary, you're going to have to realize that much of what you create is going to be on you and much of the training you receive is going to be on you.

As I've shown you above, the education system just isn't built for entrepreneurship. I've found so many of the extraordinary people that I have spoken to have focused much on self-education, either by the books they read or they work they did, outside of school. One of my favorite examples of this is Grant Cardone; someone that is totally self made through hard work, experience, and driving his own self-education.

Grant had a troubled past and struggled with drug addiction. Things that should not lead to success. He also held an accounting degree, which alone wouldn't be predictive of his massive success. However, he is currently one of the most successful entrepreneurs on the planet, with billions of dollars in real estate holdings and a very well-recognized personal brand; in addition to writing a *New York Times* bestseller.

## Grant Cardone: 10X Your Life and Experiences

Wen Grant started to tell me of his life, he began with a story from when he was eight years old. He had quarter in his pocket, which fell out and into a manhole. When he got home that night, he told his father, to which his father responded, *"Don't play with money."*

---

7. Kolmar, Chris, *AVERAGE NUMBER OF JOBS IN A LIFETIME* [2022]: *ALL STATISTICS*, 2021, https://www.zippia.com/advice/average-number-jobs-in-lifetime/

Grant then proceeded to tell the same story to his grandfather. His grandfather had been one of the coolest figures in his life. The man either had a lot of money or lost a lot of money, but he was always in action. His grandfather told him, *"The problem isn't that you lost a quarter. The problem is that you only had one quarter."*

Grant realized the solution then was that he needed to save a lot of quarters, not just depend on one. Then, at 10, something very difficult happened; his dad died. From the age of 10 to the age of 16, he watched his mom struggle for money. She worked her hardest to take care of the family, and though his dad had worked so hard to create for them during his life, they were dead broke.

## Extraordinary Story

**Brad Lea:** "Becoming a Household Name, Training Your Team Right, and Selling Bill Gates an Acura"

Brad Lea has become a household name for his viewpoints on sales as well as his ability to say whatever he means. He's a true disrupter that is consistently dropping bombs to build an extraordinary way of being.

*www.jeremyryanslate.com/lea*

The funny thing that Grant points out, though, in our society, is many people are broke. Those people are not just the poorest people—rich people and middle-class people are broke too.

Being broke can be the result of making continuous poor decisions. As people, we spend money on all the wrong stuff; that's part of the problem. Also, many of us do not know how to bring in new money. We're just effect of someone else's cause whatever someone else pays us; we'll never actually have enough. One has to figure out how to be more causative and less at the effect of the world around them.

For many Americans and people globally, one major event in their life can totally ruin them. They are not prepared for a single large financial event; they're living broke.

This gets brings us back to the problem of education. Grant mentions not being taught how to be rich by his father. This is the case for many of us; we're educated to be employees. We're educated for someone else to pay us.

Let's return to Grant's story. He was 16 years old, and his mom was clipping coupons, scared to death of losing every single dollar. She was always telling him things like, *"Turn the lights out"* or *"Don't flush the toilet."* As a youth, he hated seeing his mom scared and he had a dream to be rich.

His finances were in rough shape. Not only that; he was morally and spiritually bankrupt. He didn't have a purpose going to school. He didn't have a purpose going to college. He didn't go to school to learn all he could or to find mentors.

He didn't have a reason. He was just unfocused. He was using drugs, screwing around, wasting time, and not paying attention; just being rebellious. The thing he did right was he never quit on the dream. So when he was twenty-five, one day, after saying to himself a thousand times, *"I'm going to turn my life around,"* he said it again, and it stuck.

Grant had hated sales and quit sales jobs many times, but he made the decision "to get great at things that he didn't like." He determined that the key in getting anything he wanted was in learning to sell; all the greats could sell, and he had a desire to be great.

He decided he needed to embrace an environment around him; to make the decision: *"I'm going to get great in this environment."* Previously he had been a dilettante in sales, not taking the skills of the craft very seriously, and blaming circumstances and his surroundings rather than taking responsibility.

Rather looking just to run from the environment, always trying to change his environment by moving to another one, he decided to positively change himself to overcome the environment by getting great in it in the skills of sales. He knew that self- education was going to be the key to his success. Even more than that, like he explains in his *NY Times* bestseller, *The 10X Rule* he knew the amount of work and experience he put in would ensure his success.

He focused on just that skill and after a period of time, he became the best car salesman at the dealership. He started to break records and win more than any salesman in the area.

He had found his passion, but it hadn't started there. He had found something he was good at, and initially didn't even like, doubled down till it became effortless, and he found passion.

Before long, Grant was getting asked by others to teach them sales. It was time for his next phase of life: sales training. Grant started growing one of the most well-known sales training companies in the world.

## Extraordinary Story

**Bedros Keuilian:** "The Immigrant Edge to the American Dream"

Bedros came to America from Armenia at the age of 12. His father had a mere $20 in his pocket. His whole family lived in a tiny apartment, and he found himself digging through the trash for meals. His early years hardened his resolve and led him to create a highly successful, global brand in the fitness space.

*www.jeremyryanslate.com/bedros*

Grant started writing books. His first book, *Sell or Be Sold*, he wrote in a single weekend, and *The 10X Rule* became a *New York Times* best seller. He had become the name in sales. Then he created a new game, pushing hard into real estate and pushing his net worth over $1 billion.

As for not doing things you don't like in business, I discussed that point in my conversation with Cardone. I mentioned to Grant that I had heard a conversation he had with Gary Vaynerchuk on his *Power Players* podcast, in which Vaynerchuk stated that you shouldn't do things that you don't like to do in business.

As I previously mentioned, I take issue with Gary Vaynerchuk's advice of don't do things you hate. I was excited to hear Cardone had the same viewpoint on the issue. I love Gary. Gary's a good guy. However, Gary and I have some completely different views of a number of these things. He believes entrepreneurs can't be made; that they're genetically created.

> "Anybody can learn to be an entrepreneur. If Gary V can be a successful entrepreneur. Okay. Anybody can do it. Okay. If I can make it, dude, look, look, I own five businesses. That'll do a hundred million bucks this year. Okay. If I can do this, anybody can do it. If you want. You can. And also Gary says, you know, a God that makes Dan that makes 40 grand working for a company is better off working for himself and making the same 40 grand.
>
> I completely disagree with that. Nobody is better off making 40 grand because dude, you're in poverty at 40-K. Yeah. Okay. I don't care where you live or how you make sense. You in India, dude, you. Would appear to make you rich. The reality is you cannot move on Planet Earth with 40 grand. You can't expand, you can't grow, you can't get known.
>
> So the other thing Gary says is he doesn't do anything he doesn't like to do. That's good. Good for Gary, dude. I picked up feces

*urine. Uh, I still do it today. I do whatever I gotta do, bro. Right?*
*I'm taking care of myself, my dreams, my family, my church, my*
*community. I'll do whatever it takes. I'm never above doing."*

— Grant Cardone

The point that I'm trying to make here is that self-education and hard work, which you may not always like, is what will create real success. It's untrue that in creating success, you can just avoid things you don't like. In your process of hard work and self-education, you most likely will have to do a lot of things you don't want to. However, you will learn new skills from them and appreciation for others who will later do those things for you.

## So Good, They Can't Ignore You

For Grant, version 1.0 was not his end goal, but he knew he had to start somewhere. For you, I hope that you are selecting something that you like. For Grant, it was picking something that was available to him, even though he didn't like it.

It's understanding that this is a steppingstone and not a final destination. All too often people want to start at the top. They want to know exactly where they will end up and how they will be compensated for that.

## Extraordinary Story

**Cal Newport:** "Be So Good They Can't Ignore You"

Cal Newport is one of the most intriguing people I have ever met. He's a believer in doing "deep work," meaning projects where you just focus and block out all the noise; it's a big reason he doesn't have social media accounts. He's also a big believer that one needs to be the best and that's what makes others pay attention.

*www.jeremyryanslate.com/newport*

Grant committed to something. He found that thing that he could work on and become the best at that. Maybe it was always in the plan to be a billionaire real estate investor; maybe it wasn't. The point is, he found a place to start.

When you focus on one thing and don't get shiny object syndrome, often you can find better opportunities than you would ever know. The vital part of it is also the skills that you learn along the way.

Grant committed to something that he hated. It may not have been his purpose, but he committed. That in itself is how you find what you're meant to do in life.

Again, the sky won't open up and drop your purpose on your lap— so that you'll never have to work a day in your life. It's actually you work hard until you find out where you're meant to be, and then you get in the no effort zone; living and working in your purpose.

I read a book called *So Good, They Can't Ignore You* by Cal Newport based on a Steve Martin quote of the same idea, and it really changed my viewpoint on it. Cal had read Steve Martin's autobiography, in which he stated that the key to success was being "so good, they can't ignore you." Just like I mentioned with Mike Rowe, "Don't follow your passion, but do bring it with you."

Here's what I mean; you find something you're good at. This something should be a skill or vocation that can produce something, not some weird, pie-in-the-sky skill. Then, you continue to work at that thing until you get to the area where it becomes effortless.

That's the no-effort zone, and that's where the fun is. It's the zone where it no longer feels like you're putting in vast amounts of effort or energy; it comes more by ease. So, don't chase your passion. Work till you discover it. You'll not just be happy that you did but fulfilled in doing it.

## Extraordinary Takeaway

It's been said that many CEOs are avid readers. I like to say the extraordinary people are actually rabid readers. They consume lots of information because much of what they operate off of is not learned in school. It's learned in the School of Hard Knocks. In my experience, that's been the most effective form of education.

Many of the people I've spoken to had multiple attempts at greatness. Sometimes it wasn't the first, sometimes it wasn't the second, sometimes it wasn't even the third attempt that they got it right. Eventually, they figured it out, though. To me experience is one of the most valuable teachers. From my conversations with extraordinary individuals, it's one of the biggest things I found. They don't depend on the traditional education system, though some may have lofty degrees. If they do depend on their college educations, it's for the connections that they bring rather than the information.

To be extraordinary is to understand that much of the information that you consume that will help you to create your extraordinary work will be driven by your own desire to find it. Self-education is one of the most common things I have found of all the individuals I have spoken to—from Grant Cardone, to Kevin Harrington, to the founder of Overstock.com, Patrick Byrne. They are people that are driven by their own thirst for knowledge.

If you want to be extraordinary, you need to take responsibility for the information you consume, positive or negative. You need to be filling your head with the right information that will help you succeed, not the negative information that will scare you away from doing so.

I've found value in information by its workability. If something works for me, it has value. If something does not work for me, then it does not have value. That's why I found most of the knowledge that I've learned in school to be worth very little, because most of it can't be applied.

There are many careers in life for which you do need many years of education. Through my own life and in the conversations I've had, I have found the greatest institution to be the School of Hard Knocks.

Don't be afraid to get knocked around, like Grant Cardone, put in the work every single day, learn from every single experience, and be willing to educate yourself. You should always be seeking the information you want to learn and always trying to apply so you can quickly learn what has value to you and what does not. Don't be afraid to fail. Just make sure you're learning.

# 4. Learning from Failure

*When we are unable to love and
appreciate ourselves and our efforts, we
run away from our mistakes and failures,
rather than learning from them.*

— Meredith L. Young-Sowers

We live in a society where failure is looked down upon. This fear of failure keeps many from ever trying. However, those who are truly extraordinary have tried many things; they didn't hit a homerun on the first time at bat. They had to learn to put up with losses. And, those times they lost turned out to be some great learning experiences.

I've seen this in my own life. I've tried many things—beginning my career after graduate school as a high school teacher, starting a personal training company, selling life insurance, buying products from China and selling them on the Internet, and eventually settling on podcasting.

I don't look at these past attempts as failures but as ways to gather experience, which helped me to create what I'm currently creating.

Nick Swisher has always been my favorite baseball player. I still own a number 33 Swisher Jersey from the 2009 World Series. He played hard, he had a passion for the game, and once I really got into his story, I figured out learning from failure, working harder, and altering his approach was one of the greatest things that Nick learned how to do in his career.

## Nick Swisher: Baseball Royalty—Who Almost Wasn't Drafted

Nick Swisher's dad played for 10 years in Major League Baseball, so expectations were high for Nick. His father wasn't one of those people who ever forced him to do something, but he was an intense competitor, and that was something key that Nick learned from his father. He's also passed on his father's mindset when it comes to sports to his two daughters—not pushing them into any sport, letting them choose, and supporting them in it.

You can't force somebody to do something that they don't have a love or passion for. For Nick, he was able to love the game of baseball, and his dad just enhanced that.

He remembers when he was five years old, with his dad in Waterloo, Iowa, driving around on a bus, playing tape ball in the locker room during the games, collecting aluminum cans.

And after the game, he remembers trying to get enough money to buy his own baseball mitt. He was fortunate enough to have a father who had played on a major-league level just like he dreamed of. Nick always saw it as easier to listen to somebody who had been in those situations rather than not.

Very few people know Nick better than his dad, and his dad knows him up and down. Though his dad didn't force him to play baseball, he did force him to be the best at whatever he was doing; a powerful message for our youth.

## Extraordinary Story 🎤

**A.J. Hawk**: "Lessons from First-Round Draft Pick to Super Bowl Champion"

AJ Hawk is a former first-round pick from Ohio State University, drafted in the first round by the Green Bay Packers, with whom he won a Super Bowl. Later finishing his career with the Cincinnati Bengals. The thing that was most interesting to me about AJ was that he told me the greatest skill he learned later in his career was how to listen to his body to stay healthy on the field.

*www.jeremyryanslate.com/hawk*

We need to let today's youth know that they can do anything they want to do in this world. It takes drive, it takes sacrifice, and it takes time to get to where you want to be. Nick's dad set an expectation for him: *"I don't care if you're a baseball player or if you're a musician or you're a trash man, but whatever you're going to do, even if you're going to be a trashman, you're gonna be the best trash man in the world."*

It was an expectation that Nick was going to work that hard at his craft; that was kind of mindset that he took on. He may not be the most skilled guy out there, but it would definitely be hard to find somebody who could outwork him. That mindset led him to be a three-sport athlete in school, with an opportunity to play safety at Notre Dame.

He went on his first recruiting trip at West Virginia, a perennial top-25 football team. The size of the players led him to think that football would not be his sport.

Many professional baseball players are drafted right out of high school, then they spend three to five years in the minor leagues before they eventually make it to the majors—if they make it to the majors. Nick expected to be a first-round pick right out of high school but was shocked to find out he was not.

This was back in the days when the draft was 50 rounds; now the draft is 20 rounds. To go 50 rounds and not get drafted was a very big letdown for Nick, let alone not being a first-round pick. His senior season had been an incredible one: hitting .550, with 17 home runs and driving in 70 runs in 35 games.

That was one of the most depressing times in his life, and left him asking: *"What more do I have to do?"* It was in this very moment when Nick truly benefited from having a father that had been there and done that. He was able to check in with his dad about the current situation.

## Extraordinary Fact

- Less than three in 50, or about 5.6%, of high school senior boys interscholastic baseball players will go on to play men's baseball at a NCAA member institution.

- Less than eleven in 100, or about 10.5%, of NCAA senior male baseball players will get drafted by a Major League Baseball (MLB) team.

- Approximately one in 200, or approximately 0.5%, of high school senior boys playing interscholastic baseball will eventually be drafted by an MLB team.[8]

These are the opportunities that you get to choose. We all have the ability to choose how we react to situations. Nick always spoke about

8. HS Baseball Web Editor, *Probability Of Playing College and Professional Baseball*, 2021, http://www.hsbaseballweb.com/probability.htm

how getting knocked down in life is guaranteed to happen. It's in those moments when we don't stay down, and we learn how to get up, that we truly learn and grow in life.

When Nick reached out to his dad, he told him to pull himself up by his bootstraps; he still had an incredible opportunity to go to college and use baseball to pay for his education.

Nick went on to have an incredible career at Ohio State University. He then was drafted in the first round by the Oakland Athletics, the first pick of the Moneyball Era. In fact, today, one of the baseball fields at Ohio State University is called Nick Swisher Field.

He went from a non-drafted player out of high school to a first rounder out of college. It led him to questioning if he would really have a career as a professional ball player. For him, there was so much pride in that turn around, because of the amount of work, preparation time, and mental exhaustion that went into all that. He trained more, he showed up more positive every day and tried to be a better clubhouse leader. The experience had taught Nick the better he could help his teammates to show up, the better he would show up.

When he looks back on it, Nick looks at losing as something that really helped him appreciate how valuable winning was. It also helped Nick and his father Steve, drafted in the first round in 1973, to become one of very few father and son combinations to both be drafted in the first round. This achievement will always hold a special place for Nick and his dad.

Had he quit after high school, he never would have known what this part of the process would have been like and would have never had the opportunity to play Major League Baseball.

## Mentorship, The New York Yankees, and a World Series Champion

After several successful seasons with the Oakland Athletics, Nick found himself in a very difficult season with the Chicago White Sox. He had only hit .219, and the organization was ready to move on from him.

He was ready for a new situation, but he was also ready for mentorship. In 2009, he was traded to the New York Yankees, the winningest franchise in major league baseball. The locker room had the names of legends in it—Andy Pettitte, Jorge Posada, Derek Jeter, Alex Rodriguez, and the list goes on and on.

### Extraordinary Story

**Johnny Damon**: "From the 'Idiots' of Bean Town to the Evil Empire of NY, Winning a World Series with the Yankees and Red Sox"

Johnny Damon is a very unique player, whom I still think should be in the Hall of Fame. He is one of the few players to win the World Series with both the Boston Red Sox and the New York Yankees. The two teams have one of the greatest rivalries in professional sports. Johnny was the spark plug to a 2004 Red Sox team that helped to break a nearly 100-year drought in winning a World Series.

*www.jeremyryanslate.com/damon*

Nick was in such awe; he'd just had the worst year of his career in Chicago in 2008. All of a sudden, he has the realization: *"I'm good enough to play with these guys."* Yes, it helped him to elevate his game, but he also now had the opportunity to see how some of the greats of the game did business every single day and patterned himself after that.

He gives a lot of credit to the core leaders of the team in those years. Nick states: *"If Derek Jeter didn't want that music on, it would have been turned off 100 percent. "* Meaning he had learned, from experience, from his time with Derek Jeter, what real leadership looks like and how to create an environment for success.

In 2009, the first year of the new Yankee Stadium, the team knew they had to do something special. The importance was in the air. It took the team a long time to gel, but with leaders like the core four (Mariano Rivera, Derek Jeter, Jorge Posada, and Andy Pettitte), and the addition of Alex Rodriguez, they knew this team would be something special.

In this new situation, Nick went from feeling cursed in Chicago to blessed in New York City.

It was a new era in New York. Recently coming out of the Joe Torre era, the clubhouse had previously been a very stoic place. But with Nick's addition, and players like AJ Burnett and CC Sabathia, the energy changed; it was a major transition for the New York Yankees.

With the passing of George Steinbrenner, ownership had changed a great deal too. George's son Hal was now running the team, just as powerful as his father, but with a different way about him. For most teams, an almost 10-year gap would have been fine for the fan base, but for the New York Yankees, the fans were getting very antsy; they were ready for another World Series.

Nick started out that 2009 season on the bench. He was behind Xavier Nady, an absolutely dominant player, coming off a great year with San Diego. He drove in a hundred runs in 2008, hit 20-plus home runs, and was solid in right field. However, early in that season, Nady got hurt, and the door was open for Nick.

When he got his opportunity to get in there, Nick got a pinch hit in game one and he doubled. Then he got to pinch hit in game two and I walked. Finally, in game three, he got to start, hitting two home runs and driving in five runs. From that day on, the job was his; he was the starter in right field. A position he would hold for another four seasons.

The 2009 playoffs was the first time that Nick had been in such an environment. The thing that I was most curious about is if his preparation changed. In a previous conversation with former New York Yankee Johnny Damon, I found for Johnny it was important to always do the same thing and treat it as a regular season game. I was curious if Nick had the same approach.

The biggest struggle for Nick was not in his preparation changing, but it was in being such an emotional player. It was important for him to stay even keeled. He had a tendency to play off emotion, and that could make it very difficult for certain games.

It was a new environment; nearly 60,000 people filled the stadium every night, and the energy was off the charts. That's where Nick learned to lean back on the locker room that he had entered that year; players like Jeter and Posada had been there and had won. They helped to keep the team grounded in order to win. Those veterans were tough; they were real pros. That mentorship was vital to the 2009 playoff run.

Nick's numbers that postseason weren't very good. However, the assurance from the veterans kept him going and took his focus off numbers, and he continued to play hard. What mattered is that the team played to win the game. He learned to realize that he couldn't give up just because he wasn't playing well. His teammates were depending on him to show up; his moment could happen at any time.

It was that give and take relationship and the fact that he had leaders in the locker room—all those future hall-of-famers were able to keep the team steady, and that was key to a world championship. That was also the postseason when Alex Rodriguez finally broke out of the postseason slump; his chains were finally off, and he had some big home runs in support of the team.

Hideki Matsui won the MVP of the World Series and only played in three games. That's why Nick calls 2009 a *"magical year."*

Nick came to the Yankees looking to revive his career and in that time period became an all-star and won a World Series. Failure can be a teacher, but it can also be an opportunity for rebirth.

**Failure the Teacher and the Phoenix**

The legend of the phoenix is that it rises from the ashes; its loss is actually a birth. For Nick Swisher, the stories we looked at from his career really are stories of rebirth. They show us what can be possible if you look at failure as something you can learn from. Change your operating basis, learn how to work harder, and rise from the ashes.

Extraordinary people know that every loss is an opportunity to learn in order to win next time. It is the ordinary person who loses and gives up and does not find another opportunity from what just occurred. It is a real skill to be able to look at every situation for learning points to become the best version of yourself.

As Thomas Edison once said in his search for the correct filament for a light bulb: *"I have not failed. I've just found one thousand ways that do not work."* That is truly what greatness is—being able to continue trying, and when you don't succeed, putting in that vision so you can.

Greatness is being able to adjust to failure and use it for a launching point. There is also an element of humility as well. You have to be able to acknowledge what you did wrong or how you underestimated the amount of effort that you needed in order to make something happen. Confidence is important, but if you are overconfident, you don't look at your own shortcomings so that they can be strengthened.

To be extraordinary is not just continuing to work hard; it's also the ability to see the areas which you need to improve so that you can achieve your goals and dreams.

## 🎯 Extraordinary Takeaway

We despise failure in our society, to the point that we give others participation trophies just for showing up. In actuality, these people who received participation trophies lost; they're losers. The issue is that there's nothing wrong with being a loser, if failure is not final. However, for most people, failure is very final. The old adage goes: *"If at first you don't succeed, try, try again."* The current American adage goes: *"Well, at least, we tried..."*

Extraordinary people like Nick Swisher don't operate that way. They look at failure for what they can learn from it so that they never lose again. Failure is a way to become better; it is a way to hone your skills so that you become the best version of yourself. In actuality, champions are those that have lost more times than many of us have even tried, and that's why they later become champions. To become extraordinary you have to be willing to take the losses but not dwell on them. This is a very important point.

For many it is dwelling on the losses that actually ends their dreams. Yes, there will be losses. Figure out what you can learn from them but don't live them. You have to use them to plan for the future. It's as Nick Swisher said, *"If it wasn't for losing, we wouldn't know how great winning is."*

It's okay to be a loser at first, if you figure out how to use that to become a perpetual winner.

# 5. Done Is Better than Perfect

*Well done is better than well said.*

— Benjamin Franklin

One of the biggest things I have found about extraordinary people is their drive just to make it happen. Most of the world waits for life just to come to them; everything has to be perfect before they can take any action at all.

I have always been someone who just goes for it, as often seen by the email marketing pieces I send that usually have typos in them. I was always inspired by Grant Cardone writing his first book in a weekend. Grant had a reader email him after the fact, listing hundreds of spelling and grammar errors that were found.

Upon receiving the message, Grant just chuckled to himself. While others cared so much about spelling, he had just gotten his ideas out there.

I've found that extraordinary people just go for it and sort it out later. It will be messy, imperfect, and possibly result in a lawsuit, but they know that you have to not just grab opportunity but create it. Speed is the friend of success; we can always worry about spelling and grammar later.

Many of us constantly focus on quality. Yes, that's important and should be a given. However, it is actually speed that helps any entrepreneur create incredible levels of success.

You could have the perfect version of something, but if it takes too long and you fail to get it released, then you never have a chance for victory. Extraordinary people know that speed is what puts them in the position for victory. The results may not be perfect, it may not be pretty, but it creates results. Results can be built off of, and a better version can always be created.

Speed wins. Hesitation loses. You need to think faster, act faster, and just be faster. It is speed to market and speed of action that wins. The hesitant individual does not create victory for himself.

When I think of speed to market, I think of the story of the product MyPillow. The company was developed by Mike Lindell, a former drug addict who found God, got himself clean, and created an all-American success story. The story that follows is not an exploration of politics but one of a man who lived a life of adversity but knew he was meant for more and eventually found it.

The story that follows illustrates what can happen when someone who is at the bottom of the barrel finds an opportunity and runs with it, because, due to their struggles, they've lost the ability to care what other people think about them. It is interesting that once you stop caring more about the results you create than what other people think, there's a lot of success ahead of you.

## The "MyPillow" Guy

Though he's become a bit more controversial in the last two years, Mike Lindell is an incredible American success story. In recent years, he's spoken a lot about election fraud, not a subject to tackle in this book, but whether you agree with him or not, his story is powerful.

He overcame so much, created thousands of jobs, and has been an advocate to others suffering from drug addiction.

This is the story of a drug addict, someone who wasn't going to make it, who now employs thousands of people and has created many, many jobs.

Mike had tried all his life to be an entrepreneur. He had tried different things—a carpet cleaning business and even owning his hometown bar for a period of time.

That's when Mike became a very functioning addict—the early 90s to the early 2000s. It led him to have to sell the bar he owned for over a decade.

By that time, he had gotten into crack cocaine, and he'd become a full-blown crack addict. On a parallel track, it took about a year, he had this dream of MyPillow. He woke up and frantically wrote down the details of his plan. He knew he could have it.

His 10-year-old daughter came upstairs to his room and asked him what he was doing. He went on to tell her that he was creating the MyPillow and the change that this product would make. Incredulously, she just stared at him and sipped her water.

Mike spent about two years trying absolutely everything. He knew what he was going to create with this pillow and the problem he was going to solve. Standard pillows always went flat, which led Mike to believe this had something to do with what they were filled with.

## Extraordinary Fact

Mike, like many extraordinary people we look at in this book, is self-made. 90% of new American billionaires are self-made. Here are some figures about how the self-made stack up: [9]

9. Simovic, Dragomir, *39 Entrepreneur Statistics You Need to Know in 2021*, 2021, https://www.smallbizgenius.net/by-the-numbers/entrepreneur-statistics/

- In 2016, there were 25 million Americans who were starting or already running their own businesses.

- 46% of small business entrepreneurs are between the ages of 41 and 56.

- There are 582 million entrepreneurs in the world.

- 20% of small businesses fail within the first year.

Studies show middle-aged men start the most successful businesses.

After years of trying, Mike finally figured it out; his commitment to creating the product finally came through. He pitched the idea to many people, and they all turned him down. The big box stores wouldn't listen, the TV sellers wouldn't listen, he couldn't even get anyone to sell them on consignment. So, a friend recommended to him that he start a kiosk at the mall.

Mike set up the kiosk. It cost him quite a bit of money that he and his wife did not have. He struggled with talking to people. In addition, he was still on heavy drugs at this point in his life, to the point where getting off of them may have impaired his functioning. He made a decision that while selling at this kiosk he wouldn't do drugs, but this only lasted for a few days because he really needed the drugs to get through speaking to others.

Mike had one gentleman ask him for a business card, but at that time, he didn't have business cards. So, he found a piece of paper and quickly wrote down his phone number.

Then, a year later, Mike's phone rang. It was the gentleman that asked for a business card. He asked, *"Are you Mike from Minnesota, the guy who created MyPillow?"* When Mike responded that he was, the caller let him know that the pillow had entirely changed his life.

The caller let Mike know that he ran the Minneapolis Home and Garden Show and he wanted Mike to have a spot there to talk about MyPillow. Although he hadn't done a live show before, Mike was very excited and set up a table so he could demonstrate the pillow to all the people watching.

## Extraordinary Story

**Ted Nugent:** "Hard Work, Integrity and Sobriety; A Rock & Roll Legend's Key to Success"

The rocker of "Cat Scratch Fever" lore, Ted Nugent is a very unique musician. Ted is known more modernly for his conservative political views and hunting television shows, but he was known in the 1970's as the Motor City MadMan; a wild stage performer that has never done a drug of any kind.

*www.jeremyryanslate.com/nugent*

This was back in the days when Mike made all his own advertising. He remembers never being able to forget that first day at the Home and Garden Show. He only sold 15 pillows. However, the next day, they all came back and told him how much the product helped them. Each of those people had to pay to re-enter the show just to tell Mike how great his product was.

Mike could care less about the money. He'd only sold a few pillows, but the effect he had on others' lives lit him up.

Mike had a new way of doing things. He did live shows for about seven years. The company was starting to grow, but personally, he was falling apart. His marriage of 20 years was in the process of ending, and his drug addiction continued to get worse.

In fact, things got so bad that the people supplying him with the drugs, his dealers, decided in 2008 that it was time for them to do an intervention on Mike. At that point in time, he was staying at a hotel in downtown Minneapolis. He hadn't slept in somewhere from 10 to 14 days. He came out of the bedroom to see three of his biggest dealers.

*"We're cutting you off. You've been up for 14 days,"* one of them said to him.

Two of the men left the room, leaving just one of the dealers and Mike to speak. The man asked Mike how much crack he had left. Mike had none left and had to resort to something called carpet farming, combing the carpet and looking for anything that had fallen out of his pipe during use.

Before long, Mike fell asleep on the floor. At 2:30 a.m., Mike got up, walked down the street, and decided he was going to look for some crack. Turns out the two dealers that had left, got the word out, and Mike couldn't find anyone willing to sell to him.

When Mike returned to the hotel, the dealer was waiting for him. He said, *"Man, you've been telling us for years that this MyPillow thing is just a platform for God."*

The dealer continued to explain to Mike that he needed to do this, because when he did, he was going to come back and help the rest of the addicts. It was that thought that led Mike to later found the Lindell Recovery Network, a foundation that helps others to recover from drug addiction.

In fact, two of those dealers would later find God and begin working for Mike, proof of how strong his mission had become. However, Mike didn't actually quit in that moment. In fact, it wouldn't be until January 16th, 2009.

## Extraordinary Story

**Jeff Hoffman:** A Priceline Co-Founders #1 Billionaire Skill

The goals and vision of billionaires is what sets them apart. The thing that impressed me most about Jeff Hoffman was his ability to know exactly what to look for in an executive. As one of the co-founders of Priceline.com, it's a skill that helped him to scale a well-known global brand.

*www.jeremyryanslate.com/priceline*

That year would be a very pivotal one for Mike. He had a friend, Dick, come to him when he was at his lowest point. He was living in a rundown house in the woods, everything he owned was gone, and MyPillow was still in its nascent stages. He had always viewed Dick as his equal. They had both started using cocaine in the 80s together, which later led to crack in the early 2000s, when both men had become highly functional addicts.

Dick had found God and was excited to share with Mike. His whole life had changed; he'd been sober for a number of years. Mike began to pepper Dick with questions about the changes in his life, finding God, and getting treatment. He felt that he needed to get through the fear of everything if he would ever be able to quit.

Dick became what Mike called his "hope match," the light to help him see how he could change his life. For Mike that hope ended up being in Jesus. That day he prayed with Dick and quit all the drugs and vices. For the next two years, he focused hard on getting MyPillow off the ground and his own recovery.

Mike had the idea he needed to bring it to the people; live shows had been what had previously made him successful. He needed to figure out how to do that at scale. That's when he had the bright idea: infomercials! He started getting lots of negative feedback: *"Infomercials don't work." "You can only sell in the big box stores." "You don't have enough sales. The big box stores don't want you." "You're going to need an actor for an infomercial."* On and on it went.

Mike didn't listen to the naysayers. He just went for it. He knew that people loved his live shows, and if he could do them for more people, he could sell. So, he hired two producers from California. On one occasion, one of the producers was texting the other and happened to leave his phone out for Mike to catch a glimpse: *"This is the worst guy I've ever seen."*

*"He'll never make it on TV,"* the other responded.

To which the first said, *"He's paying you. Just humor him."*

Well, that infomercial launched October 7, 2011, in the middle of the night. Mike, some guy who was afraid of being in front of the camera, had only 10 employees at that time. Forty days later, he had 500 employees.

## 🎯 Extraordinary Takeaway

The speed with which Mike Lindell grew his company is incredible. To go from 10 employees to nearly 500 in just 40 days doesn't seem human. It shows what a little grit, and someone that is truly self-made, can do when they grasp an opportunity.

Mike thinks a big part of his success is being real. People felt like he was just like them. However, if you look closely at it, it's about more than just that. Mike had a lot of hardship in his life; this chapter could have easily fit in the one about adversity. However, the thing I want you to understand from here is that Mike had an idea, he held on to that idea, and continued to push that idea, until he found the right outlet for it. Then, once he found it, he didn't worry about how pretty it was, how perfect it was, how well written the business plan was; he just went for it.

I think sometimes we can put too much attention on just how perfect something is, and that waiting will keep us from ever getting it out there. Had Mike worried about that first infomercial and how perfect or not perfect it was, he might not have been his real self or the product may have never gotten out.

Moving forward from this, you can change your outlook on how you can get going. Don't worry so much about what it looks like. Don't worry so much about knowing everything. Just get it out there; just move forward. You can fix your mistakes later on, but you can't fix a lost opportunity.

Don't spend your time deciding if this is the opportunity or not. Just go for it. What's the worst thing that could happen? If you fail, you then have an opportunity to try again. As you'll find out later in this book, failing the first time may not be such a bad thing.

I will always be of the belief that done is better than perfect. The quick and astronomical growth of the MyPillow company is a great example of what one person, with a little drive, very little camera ability, and a big heart can make happen in just 40 days.

# 6. Create Your Own Opportunities

*To see an opportunity we must
be open to all thoughts.*

– Catherine Pulsifer

When discussing the subject of done being better than perfect, I thought I could have expanded upon that with another story. However, I realized the bigger learning point for me was that you need to create your own opportunities. So many of us wait for life to happen to us and an opportunity to show up at our front door. However, many times it doesn't happen like that. Sometimes you have to find an opening, grab the opening, widen it, and realize you are going to create the opportunity to fill that space.

Whether it's creating the want for the product you're selling or creating a niche for something that you want to sell, sometimes you have to create the demand and the space for your product.

To that effect, I have found the story of fashion designer Rebecca Minkoff to be extremely inspiring. She found her opportunity, ran with the opportunity, and created a globally recognized brand that continues to grow to this day. This is the story is of a designer with a purse and an idea that got picked up in the right place. Her idea got some media attention, which helped her to build a business. She created her own opportunity. And once she saw the attention her product garnered, she knew how to harness it, build a bigger brand, and create a global name.

## Rebecca Minkoff

For Rebecca it started at a very young age. She fell in love with the idea of creating her own items. The fact that she could think about something and then suddenly make it, was very exciting to her. Once she learned a skill, it felt very empowering. She was very thin as a youth, and so she made her own clothes since most things she bought in the store did not fit her.

Designing clothing gave her a lot of confidence. She would go to the store, buy clothing, and alter it so it fit her. It was something she loved and she wanted to continue.

As a creator, one of Rebecca's first achievements came in 2001 when she created a version of the I Love New York TV t-shirts.

## Extraordinary Fact

The "Oprah Effect" has been used for years to describe products that have launched in the TV show *Oprah*. There have been such occurrences, like Rebecca's first product getting popular from TV, of brands being recognized and started from initial media attention. Attention was created, which led to demand, and a company was born.

One example of this is the creation of Scribe Media, first known as Book in a Box, which came from author Tucker Max being interviewed on Lewis Howes' podcast, *The School of Greatness*. Great business ideas can be spawned from demand from media attention.

Here are a few products that were launched from the Oprah effect:

- Spanx
- Kindle
- UGG Boots
- iPad[10]

---

Rebecca went to the Caribbean for a trip and was inspired by the Aruba-themed shirts she saw and wanted to create one for New York upon her return. So, she cut up an I Love New York t-shirt and started wearing it around, and her sister-in-law wanted one. She was then wearing that t-shirt when having dinner with Jenna Elfman, who was a really big TV star at the time.

So, two days before the Twin Towers fell, September 9, 2001, Rebecca sent a shirt like the one she was wearing to Jenna Elfman. She then went on to wear the shirt on the *Jay Leno Show* as a sign of support to the city.

It became a buzz in the magazines, newspapers, and the early budding online blogs. So she started creating shirts and giving the profits to the Red Cross to help with the recovery effort. In fact, she spent nine months of her life on the project. She would bike down to Canal Street, make the shirts, turn around, and head back home. It's literally all she was doing at that point. It was such a huge project.

Many hours cutting, tying knots, and at some point, even getting blisters on her fingers. She wasn't making any money, but she was able to pay the rent and support the bigger mission of what was happening in New York City.

---

10. Bukszpan, Daniel, *10 Products That Oprah Made Popular*, 2011, https://www.cnbc.com/2011/05/24/10-Products-That-Oprah-Made-Popular.html

## Who Designed that? Well, I did.

Though she got early attention for the creation of I Love New York t-shirts, Rebecca Minkoff is really famous for designer handbags. How the business started is a very interesting and unique story.

Elena Cardone: "Build An Empire, How to Have it All"

## Extraordinary Story

Elena Cardone started her career in Hollywood and soon became a successful actress and model of TV and film fame. A lifelong competitive sport shooter, and best selling author, public speaker, and visionary. Elena currently hosts her own show, "Women in Power" and previously co-hosted "The G&E Show" with her husband, Grant Cardone, bestselling author, entrepreneur and real estate investor.

Together they have created a real estate portfolio of over one-billion dollars.

*www.jeremyryanslate.com/elena*

It started back in 2005. Jenna Elfman came back to her, after enjoying the T-shirt she had given her. She asked Rebecca if she designed bags. She didn't, but she lied and told her she did. Jenna informed her that she had a movie role that was coming up in two weeks and she needed a special and unique bag for the movie. Two weeks seemed like a very tight timeline, but she agreed to it and decided she would just make it happen. She scrambled like crazy, went to the garment center, found a bag manufacturer, and got two bags made. She focused on a design that she really wanted for herself, and it was for that reason she had two of them made.

She thought the bag would be great for Jenna's character. So, she shipped it, but then FedEx didn't deliver on time. They started shooting without it and they weren't willing to go back and insert the bag into the film later on. Rebecca was devastated; the opportunity seemed lost. This was the first designer bag she'd ever purchased, and now it was essentially useless to her. Should bought one for Jenna, which arrived late, and kept the second one for press. She expected press would want it from its popularity in the movie.

## Extraordinary Story

**Kara Goldin:** "Finding Success by Thinking in Solutions and Positive Outcomes"

Kara Goldin is the Founder and CEO of the Hint Water company. When she first started the company, she could not get anyone to carry her product. The way she got it into Whole Foods was to do so on consignment. Meaning, she gave the store a case and they would pay her only after the product was sold. The brand took off. In fact, she was on the phone with a distributor trying to get more of her product into Whole Foods while in the hospital giving birth to her child.

*www.jeremyryanslate.com/goldin*

It was then that Rebecca decided she would start wearing the bag around; since she had it, she would at least enjoy it. She didn't necessarily do anything at that point to get people to notice it, but someone walking down her street asked her, "Who's your bag? I love it." It made her think she may have something.

She showed it to a friend of hers, and the friend was blown away. The friend wanted to put it in her store, and get a friend of hers that wrote for the Daily Candy, essentially the only social media of the day, to write about it. The Daily Candy was a large email list that sent out the newest and hottest items of the day.

It didn't just get noticed; it got noticed in a huge way. They wrote an article called "The Cat Walk of Shame" because the bag was called the Morning After Bag. This was the pivotal moment to the beginning of Rebecca's career. It all began with someone asking her on the street who made her bag, which inspired her to go create her own opportunity.

## A Hit Product Becomes a Brand

That single bag helped Rebecca to build a very successful fashion company, recognized all over the world. Because the initial attention in Daily Candy was extraordinary, her friend's store sold out of bags. They had bought 15 units and ordered another 75. Due to the early success, Rebecca was primarily focused on fulfilling orders. She had boutiques that were interested. She had magazines that were interested. She was suddenly in demand everywhere.

There were a lot of inbound orders, and it was her goal just to service those requests. In this time, social media celebrity was starting to become important, but her goal really was just to service the inbound and not focus on creating future business.

She was just scrambling to fill orders. So, she called her dad because she was running out of cash to fund production. Her father decided he wasn't going to help her and recommended she call her brother.

She didn't have an LLC, and she didn't have a tax ID. These were things she just didn't really know about. That was when her brother came in and helped her make all those things happen. His entry into the business really was like Business 101. He could see the heat around the brand and the escalation and sales and he knew that Rebecca had quite a business ahead of her.

## 🎙 Extraordinary Story

**Dr. Brian Keating:** "Into the Impossible: A Glimpse into the Minds of Nobel Laureates"

Dr. Brian Keating may be one of the single most intelligent people I have ever met. He's a cosmologist that studied how the universe began. In fact, he was up for a Nobel Prize until his premise was proved wrong, leading him to write a book and explore further the thought process of some of the greatest minds to ever live.

*www.jeremyryanslate.com/keating*

He was really able to step in and help her formalize the business side of things. It was at that moment he became her co-founder. He's the CEO to this day. He helped to shape the business, and it made sense because she really wanted to stay out of that side of things. She wanted to stay creative, design, and be on the PR side of things.

As the brand has grown, in the last five years, she's gotten heavily involved in the business side of things. Rebecca has continued to evolve as an entrepreneur. An artist with a dream and a will to create an opportunity, seize it, and build a world-class brand.

## 🎯 Extraordinary Takeaways

Opportunity won't always come your way. Sometimes in life, just as Rebecca Minkoff did, you have to create opportunities for yourself to win. It's something great athletes have done for years, but something great businesspeople have not always received notoriety for. However, if you look at many of the extraordinary people that we have spoken to, when the door was closed to them, they didn't just wait for a new one to open. They built a new door.

To truly be successful you often have to be building new doors. As the phrase goes, "When one door closes, another one opens." That may be true in some ways. However, it makes more sense as: "When one door closes, go find or build a new door." To be extraordinary you have to be willing to see opportunities and create opportunities everywhere.

Once you realize that there's no scarcity of opportunities to win, you can concentrate on winning and creating opportunities for yourself to do so.

Moving forward, start looking at where you can create opportunities for yourself. Have you noticed something missing with your favorite product? Is there someone you really admire in the public light, that needs a solution you can create for them? Whatever it may be, start looking for where you can create opportunities; don't just wait for the door to open for you. When you can build your own door, you can truly be extraordinary.

# 7. Define Your Success. Don't Let Others Define It for You.

*Those who tell you that you cannot fly are the ones who chained themselves to the ground.*

—Sai Pradeep

Extraordinary people don't make decisions based on what others do. They don't select the life plan based on what others want. Honestly, I have great appreciation for my parents and everything they've done for me. However, I started my early life making decisions based on what would please them; what would make them happy.

I think many of us go through life this way, making decisions based on what others want for us; deciding what to do based on what we think is going to make others happy. We don't want to *"rock the boat."* It's much easier to deal with the loud voices of others than that quiet inner voice telling us we're just not happy.

Extraordinary people realize that you cannot make decisions based on what others want for you. "I'm not going to live my life for people that wouldn't die for me." It's a very true statement I've heard, and I think it accurately describes how an extraordinary person approaches life.

Think about the people who affect your decisions or push you to do things a certain way. If it came down to a life-or-death situation, would they die for you? Given that, do you really think it makes sense to live for them?

Now this may seem like a selfish way to think about this, but I don't mean that you should just forget everyone else in your life and go for what you want. What I mean is if you're going to live this life, you have to have some sense of enjoyment and fulfillment.

As I stated earlier, I don't think you should always be on this quest to find your life's purpose. However, you should enjoy what you do in your life and not do it because others want it for you.

To me one of the best examples of someone that is truly extraordinary got famous just for doing commercials. You may know him as the most interesting man in the world, but in real life his name is Jonathan Goldsmith.

## Your Definition of Success

If you're like me, you're a big fan of Internet Movie Database (IMDb). You look through different movies and commercials and you see what other movies people have done before. When looking up Jonathan Goldsmith, I noticed one glaring issue with his IMDb account. He had done hundreds of movies in the 60s and 70s, and then seemingly disappeared until he re-emerged as the most interesting man in the world in the early 2000s.

Many people asked him, *"You found success late in life. How do you deal with that?"* Jonathan didn't really see it that way. He had many small roles, hundreds in fact, and he just couldn't seem to break through to that next level; he wasn't getting that larger role.

He spent a lot of time on television, and he got to what was the top pay level for television actors.

Jonathan said, *"To hell with it. I'm going to just take off and go fishing."* He had decided that he was done with the Hollywood world and would try his hand at creating success in business. He got into network marketing, and the company's vision intrigued him. The product was revolutionary and before its time. He did very well, becoming the president of the company.

He was selling a marvelous product that really started waterless technology; it allowed one to do things such as washing a car without the use of water. The world was running out of water, and he built a huge company and was very successful. He was presenting all over the world. When he stood on those stages, he felt like he was an actor again and knew someday he'd go back to it.

## Extraordinary Fact

Though Jonathan Goldsmith did find success early in life, people outside of Hollywood weren't aware of it. Given that, they had decided he had success late in life; in actuality, they were just missing information.

However, there may be some reading this book that haven't had that success yet. I want to share a list I found from *Entrepreneur Magazine*,[11] as well as list from Digital Information World,[12] about people who found success later in life:

- Leo Goodwin, GEICO, founded the company at 50 years old.

---

11. Patel, Sujan, *Success Can Come at Any Age. Just Look at These 6 Successful Entrepreneurs,* 2015, https://www.entrepreneur.com/article/241346

12. Digital Information Editor, *8 Entrepreneurs Who Started Late and Found Success,* 2018, https://www.digitalinformationworld.com/2018/10/8-entrepreneurs-who-started-late-and.html

- Harland Sanders, KFC, founded the company at 62 years old.

- Ray Kroc, McDonald's, founded the company at 52 years old.

Just because it hasn't been your time yet, don't be discouraged. Just as these men did, you define your success, and there's no timeline as to when you will get it. Keep pushing.

---

After a great run, Jonathan's company ended up folding, and he ended up moving on. What made him famous for being the most interesting man in the world after that period of his life was really just true serendipity.

Even though he put his dream on layaway to go out and make some money, he came back to find it.

## Yes, Now! Figure It Out Late; Just Don't Fall Off the Horse.

The thing that I had found most interesting about Jonathan Goldsmith is that he went from being a stage actor in Brooklyn to a garbage man turned actor in Los Angeles. He became someone everyone recognized in LA.

It was important to me to learn what type of drive takes a person from one coast all the way to another in order to chase a dream. Further, I was curious about the type of person who, when that dream ends, takes a hiatus, prepares himself, and gets back to finding that dream.

Jonathan had done a picture in New York City after doing most of the local television. He was told by some people that he respected, *"Hey, you should go to California. We'll help get you some introductions."*

Jonathan had reached that point, that point when it looked like he had done all he could in the current game, and the only way to win was to seek a new game. He felt like he had done all he could do on local television. So he packed everything up and made the move to California. The new location did not give him the reception he expected. In fact, he had to work very hard just to even get noticed. So, for a period of time, he drove a garbage truck. That's when he realized big breaks are made, not given.

Well, Jonathan got a job. His first show was *Perry Mason*. He did an appearance on *Gunsmoke* after telling the director that he could ride like the wind; he had never been on a horse in his life, and he damn near fell off! From there, he started to do television and did quite a lot of television. In fact, before his good fortune with a Dos Equis campaign, he had guest starred in over 350 shows, but nobody really knew him.

He was respected by his peers and a very good journeyman actor, but the Dos Equis campaign really put him on the map.

The thing I find impressive about Jonathan is even before having his big break, he had the confidence he would have that big break. Not just the confidence, but the *swagger*; the ability to carry himself and speak in such a way that instilled confidence in others that he could do something he had probably never done before.

Part of what made Jonathan so successful was that he never really turned anything down. It didn't matter what it was: trapeze, high jumps, falls, deep water—even doing a campaign for a hair tonic company. If he didn't know it, he had confidence he could learn it, and that confidence was what carried him.

Jonathan went as far as to say that he could jump off a train and if he broke both legs, well, he'd still be ahead. At that time, he was still driving the garbage truck, so he would always have a change of clothes with him to get to his next act.

Once such experience was a big break for Jonathan. A director was looking for someone with horse skills, which he did not have, but he assumed as he had done previously, he could just agree and figure it out later.

Jonathan arrived in the office to try out for the part and observed a unique scene ahead of him. In the acting world, it was what was called a cattle call—where a bunch of people gather to try their hand at getting a part. But when he arrived, the office was empty. It appeared as he though he was the only one trying for a part. The secretary handed him his script. Jonathan asked what the "sides" were. In the acting world, sides are who you're playing in the script. The secretary told him he just needed to be himself.

## Extraordinary Story

**Frank Zane:** "A 3X Mr. Olympia on The Golden Age of Bodybuilding and Creating a Legacy"

Frank Zane is one of the only individuals to beat Arnold Schwarzenegger in the Mr. Olympia content. His type of training and aesthetic look inspired an entire generation of bodybuilders.

*www.jeremyryanslate.com/zane*

*"Mr. Daniels just wants you to be you,"* the secretary of stated. There was nothing for Jonathan to do other than to be himself. The director walked in and asked Jonathan one question: *"Are you at liberty?"* ("At liberty" meaning free or available).

Jonathan took a long pause before he answered the director. He had been at liberty ever since he arrived in California. "Yes, sir."

The director stated: *"We're delighted to have you, and we're shooting in two weeks."*

Jonathan turned around to excitedly leave and call his father, who had been heavily invested in him getting an acting job in Hollywood.

Just as he was about to turn and walk, the director asked, "Do you ride?"

Without hesitation, Jonathan replied: "Like the wind." However, he had never ridden on a horse in his life other than when his grandmother put him on a pony in Central Park. Jonathan became nervous about this part in the script. His character, Kyle, he read, "vaults" onto a horse and gallops off into the wind. *"Vaults,"* he thought to himself. He couldn't even get on a horse.

On a crisp October day, he went out to the ranch where they were filming. He sat there wondering how he was supposed to vault onto a horse and gallop off into the night. *"What am I supposed to do?"* he thought to himself. There was a semi-trailer next to where he was sitting, and he could hear a lot of noise going on. *"Oh, Wrangler, what's the ruckus going on in there?"* Jonathan said.

The wrangler said, *"It's the horses. They just want to run."*

Jonathan started preparing himself for a heart attack.

They got Jonathan up on the horse, and the horse took off. Everyone around was yelling: *"Turn them around! Turn them around!"* Jonathan was supposed to ride off into the night but instead kept riding in a circle around the cameraman. To which the director stated: *"Like the wind, huh?"* However, that ability to just go for it left him doing another 16 episodes of *Gunsmoke* and other Westerns.

Jonathan finally learned to ride on the set of a film called *The Virginian*. He almost got killed on the horse, and the stuntman walked up to him and said, *"I've never seen an actor come closer to getting killed."* The horse had reared up under an overhang, and Jonathan's back hit the roof, almost leading to catastrophic injury. That stuntman happened to be the stuntman for Gary Cooper, and went on to teach Jonathan how to ride a horse; it was the set up for a lifelong friendship between the two.

I think the greatest lesson that there is from Jonathan Goldsmith is that even if you don't know everything, that doesn't mean you shouldn't try. You should make sure that you're physically safe in most circumstances, but doubt or lack of experience shouldn't stop you from creating and trying new things. It's that same outlook that led him to the most important part of his life.

## I May not Always Act, but When I Do, I Stay Interesting

When Jonathan finally got back into acting, he couldn't find an agent. Finally, he met a woman at a boutique agency outside of LA. He felt lucky that she was willing to take him on. That agent, Barbara, would later become his wife.

To this day, Barbara still sets up a lot of his appearances. She was a very successful agent for a long time, in her own right, working with people like Shirley Jones and other well-known stars.

One day, she called Jonathan when he was living in the Sierra Mountains where he owned a ranch and some land. She let him know that they were looking for somebody for a commercial—sort of a Hemingway-type character and someone with great improvisational acting skills. It was for Dos Equis. Jonathan was a bit hesitant to even try to get the role. He believed that he did not fit the role, partially due to age, partially due to the description.

## Extraordinary Story

**Don Felder:** "A Rock 'N' Roll Legend on the State of American Rock 'N' Roll"

Don Felder described an unreal scene to me; as a member of the Eagles, he played in front of the United Nations. Though the crowd did not all speak English, they joined the band in singing the song that he had helped to write so many years before.

*www.jeremyryanslate.com/felder*

---

He drove down in his old truck, sleeping in that same truck in the campground parking lot, with no water access, just across the street from the old Malibu Colony.

You could hear everyone in the Malibu Colony enjoying themselves from just the other side of the street. At that time, he had a lot of self-doubt. When you've been out of the business for ten years, it's natural to question if you ever really had it.

The next morning, he called Barbara to try and bow out of the audition. She talked him into continuing to go for it, telling him he was *"perfect for it"* and he would *"never forgive himself if he didn't go for it."*

When he arrived for the tryout, there were maybe three, four, or five hundred people waiting in line, all handsome young Latinos. He began questioning if he was even at the right tryout.

He once again called Barbara. *"Barbara, I don't have a shot."*

To which she responded, *"Damn it, just stay there and show them what you got."* From that moment, Jonathan's only purpose was to make the people watching his audition laugh.

He would finish every statement he made in that audition with the following line: *"And that's how I arm wrestled Fidel Castro."*

While he was waiting in line, he had proceeded to take one of his socks off. His turn came up, and he did not have the chance to get his sock back on. The director asked him, *"Why is your stock off?"*

Not knowing what to do, he just went with it and responded, *"It's an icebreaker. You asked me the question, didn't you?"*

The director and the client proceeded to laugh, which encouraged Jonathan even more, and he carried on with them in a heavy Hispanic accent.

## Extraordinary Fact

He wasn't a Spanish billionaire. No, he couldn't "speak French . . . in Russian." He was just another Jewish kid from Brooklyn. Back in the late 1970s and early 80s, in between shifts as a garbage man, he was a B-list actor on *Gunsmoke, Magnum, P.I.* and *The A-Team.*

Introduced in 2006, the most interesting man in the world quickly became popular and nearly dethroned the king in the can (Budweiser). In a market dominated by domestics, the imported lager posted solid sales numbers for more than a decade.

And while other foreign imports struggled, Dos Equis' profits increased by 34.8 percent from 2007 to 2015, according to *USA Today.*

It was the pitchman's personality that "won the lifetime achievement award . . . twice." A Steve McQueen-type rolled into a modern Simon Bolivar caricature, his Spanish accent was exaggerated, but his attitude was genuine.

The most interesting man in the world has even earned the most coveted millennial stamp of approval — he's become an Internet meme.[13]

While he was carrying on and having a good time, Jonathan remembered his truck was parked illegally, and he began to worry about getting a ticket. That led him to pick up the pace remarkably fast, trying to finish with a story about having an affair with Fidel Castro's mistress.

---

13. Wegmann, Philip, *Firing the 'most interesting man' means disaster for Dos Equis,* 2016, https://nypost.com/2016/03/25/firing-the-most-interesting-man-means-disaster-for-dos-equis/

This allowed him to finish his audition with, of course, a story about arm wrestling with Fidel Castro.

Jonathan didn't hear anything about the audition for two months after that. It turns out the director and the client had gone all over South America doing auditions and couldn't find anyone as good as Jonathan. However, they remained stuck on one point: they thought the most interesting man should be a younger character than Jonathan.

One day, the casting agent called Barbara and said, *"We loved him. We really loved him. The problem is we feel like he's a little too old for the part."*

To which Barbara responded: *"How could the most interesting man be young? How could he have all that life experience?"*

The casting agent called back 10 minutes later. Jonathan had the part. The rest is history. In fact, the commercial led to him being so famous that he moved out of LA and to Vermont to get a little bit of peace in his life.

He had become famous promoting someone else's product at what looked like a later point in life with a lot of living in between.

## Extraordinary Takeaway

You're never going to have everything figured out in life. That's just not how it works. For someone to be extraordinary, they really must have the drive to keep working at it until they figure it out. They may not know exactly what they want to do, but they know they have big goals for their life.

Reading this, you can approach it like this: sometimes we'll take one step forward and two steps back, but the goal is to keep moving forward.

Don't worry that you don't have it all figured out. Sometimes you have to agree to things that you're not 100 percent confident in doing. But your goal should be to keep striving forward and never be kept in a place where you're not growing.

Not caring what other people think is probably the single hardest thing to do. We're taught by TV, social media, and other entertainment to be concerned with what others think of us. Magazines have their most popular celebrities, and in school we even vote for the most popular student. We're taught to live on praise.

However, if you truly want to be extraordinary, you cannot live on praise. There are going to be periods of time where not only is there no praise, but you're facing true hatred for what you're doing. You have to understand where that's coming from. Often, people hate you or are unhappy with you because they fear what you are doing. If you were to achieve what you are attempting to achieve, then they would think less of themselves. They're not willing to take the same risks or go to the same level of achievement you are.

The only way they can win is to tear you down. Knowing that, you need to proceed forward, not worrying what others think of you and how they feel about you. That doesn't mean you should walk around like an inconsiderate jerk—it just means that you can't let the opinions of others alter the choices you make in life. As long as you're making ethical choices that do not hurt others and for the greater good of others, then it doesn't really matter what other people think about you.

Don't let the opinions of others stop you from being extraordinary. Reach for the stars, and once you've hit them, drive past the heavens.

Don't let the limits of others be the limit for you.

Be more.

# 8. Past, Present, and Future Vision

*The most pathetic person in the world is someone who has sight but no vision.*

— Helen Keller

As entrepreneurs we're all just a little bit crazy. We walk into a room, we take a look at all the inefficiencies, and we decide how we could take that business and make it even better. We have to really keep ourselves away from shiny objects and focus on just creating our own thing rather than getting pulled into all the other things out there. It's a gift and a curse to be able to see opportunities in absolutely everything.

However, as an entrepreneur you need another level of skill to really be successful and to really create a wonderful future.

You need to be able to look into the future and make assumptions based on the past and present. For example: "How are we going to make payroll?" "How are we going to grow the business over the next six weeks? Six months? Six years?"

As an entrepreneur, you have to have the incredible ability to not just look at the future but to be the one willing to put it there. I think recent events of the last year have really made this more difficult for a lot of us.

Recently, the governor of New Jersey, where I live, Phil Murphy, got caught talking about not pushing a vaccine mandate until after the election.

Obviously, he was doing this privately because he did not want independents and undecided voters to not vote for him. And that led me to really have an epiphany. Up to that point, I had been very consumed in the political situation of the planet.

It really helped me to realize that politicians don't really care about you. Honestly, it's really a distraction. It's important to continue to be apprised of the situation so that you understand what's happening out there and can take control and not be affected by it, but as an entrepreneur, things like this can pull at us and make it so that we can't move forward. That's why it's so important to be able to project into the future and not let our present circumstances affect us in a negative way.

That's why you have to be incredibly focused on moving forward and creating a future, because that really is how we survive. It also means you have to have a really good BS filter.

## Jayson Waller

Jason Waller couldn't even spell the word "entrepreneur." However, after years of work, he would eventually win EY's Entrepreneur of the Year award. Apparently, it doesn't matter what you can spell; it just matters how hard you're willing to work to get there.

Jayson's parents were blue collar. His dad worked for AT&T on third shift and second shift. He was a union sort. His mom worked in a bakery at a grocery store, decorating cakes.

They didn't have a lot; they had enough. His family was a little poorer than middle class. His dad had an opportunity to go into business with a friend of his who had video stores when they were cool. This was right before Blockbuster, when video store business was novel and exciting.

His also had an opportunity to open up a sub shop and bakery next door for Jayson's mom. His dad's friend offered him this opportunity, when Jayson was 14, but his dad got scared, and he played it safe. He didn't want to take the risk and lose.

His father started worrying about the family. He had two younger kids, one of which had asthma. His father still had another 10 years left at AT&T before retirement, so rather than start that business, he transferred to North Carolina, where he bought a trailer and they moved into a trailer park.

Jayson was uprooted and forced to move into a new situation where he wasn't accepted. *"Southern hospitality is BS,"* he remarked. He would eventually have a lot of friends, but for many people he met, it was about how much money you had. They'd ask questions like: *"Where do you live? How much money do you make? Why do your parents live there?"*

Jayson experienced culture shock in the South and felt frustrated. He had started life in Phoenix, Arizona, where he had been the voted most popular in his eighth-grade class.

He lived in a trailer. He had that going against him. He had fake Tommy Hilfiger. He had that going against him. When he finally got his license, he got a car that cost less than most people would pay to go out to dinner; people were making fun of him, and he wasn't used to it.

He was used to being perceived as cool just by being himself. Status had nothing to do with being able to fight, or the girls he dated, or the sports he played. He could do all those things, but not having money was not something that he could overcome. Every single day, he just watched his father play it safe. This was something that in adulthood his always kept in mind; his kids are watching him.

## Extraordinary Story

**Vick Tipnes:** "The Key Components to Next-Level Success"

Vick Tipnes lost everything and doubted everything he thought was true. He invested in himself and started a small company called Blackstone Medical Services. The company grew rapidly and became the multi-million dollar brand of his dreams.

*www.jeremyryanslate.com/vicktipnes*

He always told himself if that horse came by, then he would jump on. He would never be the one that was scared to take chances; he would play to win. He was always focused and he put that mentality into anything he did, whether it was sales or the business he started.

He bounced around high schools. He never did drugs. He just got kicked out for getting into fist fights and arguing. He had a problem with authority figures because he felt like he was meant for greatness and he just wasn't getting there. He felt there was so much he needed to do; he just didn't like others' control over what and how that would be.

As a teen, Jayson started getting into the workplace, but he quickly realized that it wasn't a fit for him. He figures he had about 26 jobs before he was 25. He very quickly decided that if he was going to be a success, then he was going to have to figure out a way to work for himself. Like many extraordinary people, he found that the personality that makes you successful also makes you unemployable. You get to the point where you know what you want in life, so compromising to the demands of an employer becomes almost impossible.

He had a job at a bank and a fake ID that said he was 22 instead of 18, not because he wanted to buy booze, but so he could work. He even added to his resume that he had a two-year degree so they would take him. Jayson was making $65,000 a year at 18, when he really should have been a senior in high school. Jayson very quickly rose to be the bank's number one salesperson, but his secret got out. However, he had become such an important part of their revenue model that they kept him on. The impressive part about it is that this wasn't a small bank. He was number one in their massive call center.

That kind of attention made the young man see that there was so much more out there. Jayson began to realize he was really good and knew he had a purpose to do something bigger and better. He wanted more than the life his parents had lived.

He doesn't see it as an insult to his parents, but he wanted more. He didn't want his kids to experience what he had; he wanted to give them better. He recalls helping his father deliver newspapers in the middle of the night all for $125 a week. His dad worked hard, but that isn't the type of behavior he wanted his kids patterning.

Jayson knew that no one would outwork him. He may not have been the tallest or the fastest or the strongest, but he knew no one would work as hard as he was willing to work. He could grind it out like no one else was willing to and would bring more passion to the table too.

He learned, as many extraordinary people have, that he had this desire, this need, and this want to do something different. The trouble came in figuring out how to channel that energy. What Jonathan eventually put out into the world of solar technology is extraordinary, but his first version wasn't nearly as big and as impressive.

Extraordinary people tend to suffer more than others with something we like to call *"shiny object syndrome."* It's a disease where everything just looks so good, it could be the ticket to making it big. We may run, as my dad likes to say, "from pillar to post," or from one opportunity to the next. We're afraid we may miss that thing or that we have to have so many irons in the fire. The truth is, as I've mentioned earlier, you just have to pick something and commit. Then, once you have success, you can start branching out into other opportunities, in addition to coming up with better ideas and getting better at delegating. You have to get one that runs and produces revenue consistently first. It's easier said than done. We've all been there. It's a life lesson that you learn from experience. What you commit to may not be the sexiest opportunity, but your instincts tell you it will produce revenue. In fact, more often than not, the least sexy opportunities are the ones that produce the most consistent revenue.

The question is, how do you decide which area to commit to? There are so many shiny objects you can chase.

The first business Jayson opened up was in home security. He was still in high school, and he was telemarketing on the phone for a home security company. The strategy goes like this—he would call and say:

> *"Hey, Jeremy, you remember hanging out in the mall and registering to win that Dodge Durango? Great news, you're still in the running for that, but you've actually been selected to win a free home security system installation; equipment's free. The only thing you have to pay for, Jeremy, is a dollar a day for the monitoring. It keeps the bad guys away, and if you fall and can't get up, you're going to be protected. When can I schedule an installer to come out and do that?"*

He was doing that at 16 and 17 years old in high school and crushing it. So he knew when he opened up a home security business at around 24 years old, he could make it happen. Besides, he had a bone to pick with corporate America. He wasn't getting promoted—maybe because of his age, or his personality, or maybe he just wasn't polished enough. He had raw talent—he could sell, and he was hungry—but he wasn't refined yet.

When he opened up his first business selling home security, he started in a bedroom with a tile board from Home Depot that you buy for 12 bucks. He put it on the wall, grabbed a Sharpie, and wrote down the schedule. He would go to Verizon, where he was an account manager, and work all day.

He would sell Blackberries to companies and tell them, *"This is the future. You're not going to use your landline or a fax machine anymore."*

Though they were incredulous, the companies would purchase from him in droves. He had believed it was the future, and he could get them to see it. It was a unique talent he possessed that would guide him in each business he did. His home security business grew very quickly, and within nine months, he was able to quit his job at Verizon and focus exclusively on his business.

One day, he finally got an office. He grew the company and managed to make it effortlessly produce profit. But, like most extraordinary individuals, he got bored and wanted to do something else. He had sold home security systems for 10 or 12 years and made a lot of money doing it. He started looking for his next shiny object. He had a feeling that the industry was going to start slowing down, and he wanted to find something he felt had an eye to the future and would help him to grow to a new level.

## Extraordinary Story

**Jack Canfield:** "Building Your Life on the Principles of Success"

Jack Canfield and his co-author, Mark Victor Hansen, pitched *Chicken Soup for the Soul* to hundreds of publishers, and no one wanted it. They trusted in themselves enough to make it happen, and the book series has become one of the best selling of all time and a movement all its own.

*www.jeremyryanslate.com/canfield*

His home security business had done about $12 million in revenue. To grow more he partnered with another home security company that had done about $18 million. In their first year, the new company did about $38 million in sales. They ran into a problem: there were too many cooks in the kitchen; no one was really in charge. Jayson was a type-A personality, his new partner was a type-A personality, so you can just kind of see how this thing went. In 2015, they had a conversation. Jayson decided to leave home security. His partner would stay, and Jayson would take a buyout. That was when he decided to take his chance and take a run at the solar industry.

He'd heard a lot of people on the West Coast and the Northeast talking about solar in the years leading up to his departure from home security.

He loved everything about solar. It was green and clean, it eliminated the monopolies of the power companies, and it allowed consumers and companies to control their own costs. Something about that reminded him of the cell phone business; it felt very futuristic.

When he had first got into the cell phone business, around 2001 or 2002, only about 30 percent of consumers had a cell phone, and most people still had landlines. He was eager to dive into solar and very interested in how it worked. To most people, solar seemed foreign, almost like an alien invasion. For Jayson, someone who had always jumped in with both feet, he knew if he could just learn this, he could make it big.

Jayson was confident he could sell ice to Eskimos, and if he could just learn enough about solar, it could be a game-changer not just for his income but the impact he could make globally. Years one and two, he lost a ton of money. He had to sell his house and didn't get a paycheck. He put all the money he made in his home security business back into solar to try to make it work.

From talking with many extraordinary individuals, I've seen how important it is to be in alignment with something. More specifically, it's alignment with what you enjoy and your own core values that's important. It only makes sense that in Jayson's case, he would go from selling cell phones, to selling home security systems, to eventually ending up in solar power. Those things all have an eye toward the future; they all have a bent towards the advancement of technology.

Just because you're excited about a business, and you have some income saved up from previous experience, doesn't mean it's going to be easy. In fact, you're still probably going to take your lumps. You have to be willing to get through those tough times. They will be there, but it's from those moments that you can learn to scale. For many founders, the first thought is: *"When do I get that paycheck?"* If they're venture-backed, they get it right away, not even considering whether or not they've brought a viable product to market yet.

However, when you're doing it yourself, you're not funded; it's all based on what you have and what you can create. Then, if you don't bring a viable product to market, and quickly, you won't survive. Self-funded companies that don't sell in quantities fast enough go extinct.

In Jayson's first year, because he had that lump sum of money from the sale of the solar business, and he had a house pretty much paid for, he didn't need a paycheck.

He expected to crush it right out of the gate, but that didn't happen. Year one, they lost a million dollars. Somewhere around year two, he had to sell his house on the lake. The company was losing money, he'd sold his house, and now his family was starting to lose faith in him. His wife was demanding that he figure out what to do. For the first time in his life, he felt like he was actually going to lose. Up until that point, he had trained himself to win. Now things were going in the wrong direction, and he really didn't know how to right the ship.

He was the type of guy who would do whatever it took to win. The problem was, in this situation, he didn't know what to do to turn things around. If he had just one thing he could point to and one thing he could change, then he could do something about the situation. The current situation left him paralyzed.

His back was up against the wall. He was at the point when he ran out of money. That's when he sold the house and reinvested that money into the business. It felt like things had gotten very real, more real than they'd ever been before. He let all his staff go and went back to the things that he knew worked when he had built that first home security business.

He started learning about everything: permits, design, structural engineer stamps. He started doing everything: customer care, making sales calls, and running the sales appointment. In fact, in the middle of a sales appointment, just to give himself some additional credibility, he said *"Let me put you on hold and talk to my manager."* After which he picked up the phone and said what needed to be said to close the sale.

The beautiful thing about Jayson's story is how it exemplifies one of the most important principles of entrepreneurship: you may not need to do everything at your company, but you need to know how it all works. If you know how it all works, then you know how to fix it all, and you can't be taken advantage of by hiring a bad agency or employee. In this case, Jayson established his company so he knew how it all worked and saved himself a lot of money when things were tough by doing it all himself. I can imagine during that bootstrapping phase that his brain cells didn't much like trying to be in all of those places at once!

He was the one writing the checks. But guess what? He didn't have to pay anyone sales commission because he was the one doing the deals. The company was now more profitable because he was bootstrapping. He had gotten back to the things that worked when he built that first company, not new things he hadn't tried yet.

By 2016, he was back on payroll and building a new team below him. By 2017, the momentum had grown, and he closed the deal in their second state. He also closed the deal for their first NFL stadium with the Detroit Lions. Then they switched to American solar panels, and the company doubled in size overnight. In fact, they did $380 million in sales in 2019 and in 2020 were on target to surpass $750 million. For Jayson, growth like this doesn't just mean the company's worth more; it means the employees are worth more; it means the stock is worth more. They're all trying to grow the business, but it all started with him finding the right leverage to get through it.

## Make Decisions for the Future, not Stuck in Right Now

Just as Jayson did with Verizon and later having income from his home security business, I'm a big believer in building your business while you already have something else. This is where the idea of having a future vision for an entrepreneur fits in; being able to look to the future but not getting stuck in the right now because you desperately need to make money. When you have to do that, you make a lot of bad decisions.

A person can make a lot of short-sighted decisions when he needs money. It might come down to *"I need three hundred bucks this week just to eat Top Ramen,"* even though your company could make $3 million in a year's time. You need to be able to make that decision and look into the future. That's why it's really important to have something else while you're building your thing. For me and for Jason, it was a job.

When you make decisions in fear because you need money, you don't make ones with an eye to the future. If you've already got that money and you don't have to pay yourself, you make wise decisions to grow the company and you reinvest in the company.

As Jayson puts it:

> *"If you open a business, people think: 'Shoot, I'm gonna open a business. I might have all these nice cars.' No, you don't get paid. You're paid the least amount for a long time. You've gotta be ready. Like you said, you eat ramen and SpaghettiOs—that's it. If you want dessert, get bread and cinnamon and sugar and shuffle that stuff up in a ball—that's dessert."*

## Extraordinary Fact

Jayson's story is more common than not. According to Bloomberg, many successful entrepreneurs did not find success until their second attempt.

It would seem that the idea that experience plays well to winning is quite true.

*"To understand how these enterprises fare, Francine Lafontaine and Kathryn Shaw studied the successes and failures of retail entrepreneurs in Texas from 1990 to 2011.*

*Over the 21-year-period, 2.4 million retail businesses opened and 2.2 million closed. Three out of every four were founded by first-time business owners.*

*Lafontaine and Shaw found that the Texas retailers were less successful than the national average for small businesses: One in four closed after a year; half after two.*

*What happened next was telling. Of the first-time entrepreneurs whose businesses closed quickly, the overwhelming majority—71 percent—didn't bother to try again. But the tenacious 29 percent who did were more likely to be successful the second, third, and even tenth time around. Somewhat paradoxically, their success rate increased with their number of past failures."* [14]

It seems as though tenacity and experience can be the best traits to have for success.

Jayson knows from experience, he's been there, and he will be the first to tell you about how much of a struggle it really is. He was lucky enough to have his Verizon job for the first one, and then a little bit of money in the bank for the second one.

Then, he had more money in the bank for the third one until it all ran out. Just when he was ready to call it quits, that's when it all worked out. It was then that Jason made four smart rules for himself on how he would operate his business. Number one: pay your people

14. Bloomberg Editor, *Failed Entrepreneurs Find More Success the Second Time*, 2014, https://www.bloomberg.com/news/articles/2014-07-28/study-failed-entrepreneurs-find-success-the-second-time-around

first. Number two: pay your vendors next. Number three: reinvest in the business. Finally, number four: if there's anything left after that, that's what you take home.

I have found this rule to be very true myself. When I first started my current company back in 2016, it had a different name and a different set of founders. We had grown very quickly and had a six-figure business from nothing in under six months. At that point in time, in addition to the three founders, we had one employee who still works with me today.

Though it was a fast nine months of growth, we all decided we wanted to go in different directions; that was the end of the company. My wife and I had been two of the co-founders, and we decided to continue what we were doing and start a new company. We convinced the one employee we had to continue working with us. At that time, we had only liabilities and no income. We were still servicing clients who had signed up with us under the previous business name and had already paid for their services.

We had no income for about three months while I tried to put everything back together. I also took freelance work to pay for employee salaries and vendors, but I didn't pay myself. I've always remembered that, and because of that I remind myself I will never allow that to happen again. However it brings up an important fact: always pay your people first because good people are hard to find.

When you're following the four rules that Jason has and you're paying all of your vendors and staff, then you can actually make decisions for the growth of the company, not the bills you have to pay this week. Yes, there should be a demand for income from the company's founder, but the company needs to exist in order to fill that need for income.

## Extraordinary Takeaway

Looking to the future when you're trying to survive day to day can be the hardest skill to learn. When you want to be successful as an entrepreneur or a visionary of sorts, then it's a skill you have to master. When you are stuck in surviving right now, you can't see three inches front of your face; there's no way you can see the future.

That's why it's best to have a job while you're building something or to have a first business running before you build a second. When you're not making decisions based on eating this week and instead focusing on the growth of your company and looking towards the future, then you can truly create a future.

I'm a believer that artists create the future that most of us can't see yet. Well, in a way, powerful entrepreneurs like Jayson are artists. They've managed to figure out how to not get stuck in the past or the present so that they can be the ones to put the future together for us. If you are living in yesterday or even in the here and now, there's no way you can create what's not here yet.

Moving forward, you need to learn how to look at the future and plan and think in the future. When you do that, you can create incredible amounts of success. When you're stuck in past failures or an eternal present, you will never create the future.

Extraordinary people put the future first; ordinary people fight their past and try to survive in the present.

Be the one that builds the future.

# 9. Be the One to Tell Your Story
## (Because No One Else Will Do It for You)

*There is no greater agony than bearing
an untold story inside you.*

— Maya Angelou

N o one will ever tell your story for you. In fact, most people will never look for you story. This is not to invalidate your story or the power of it but rather to teach you an important lesson: you must become your own evangelist.

The best way to help you to understand this concept is to tell you a brief story. For me, telling stories is my life's purpose. Stories of the past may have been what compelled me to get my master's degree in history, and now, whether it is through my podcast, *Create Your Own Life*, or through my public relations firm, Command Your Brand, I work with stories. For me, stories have always held tremendous power.

In the early days of my PR agency, I was our first salesperson. I had a conversation with someone on LinkedIn who was just starting to grow their business. The individual was a functional medicine doctor, something I believe that we need a lot more of.

As new connections often do, the individual sent me a LinkedIn message to ask me about what Command Your Brand does. I responded *"Well, for individuals like yourself, to help tell their story through the power of podcasting."*

The response that I received was quite odd: *"I'm going to keep working on my business till I get to a level of success that the media notices me."*

I was shocked. Most people believe the lie: do good work, and eventually, you'll get noticed. While that sounds nice in theory, it's just not how the real world works.

The media does not look for you. It's a sad truth. There's no one going around looking for all the good things happening in the world. The more news you watch, the more you'll learn that the media just looks for bad things and the things that scare you. It's their purpose. So, if you are going to use their powers for good, then you have to learn the right way to play the game.

## Extraordinary Fact

A study by the *Atlantic*,[15] when looking at videos and stories published daily, found that the *Washington Post* published 500 per day, the *New York Times* pushed 230 per day, the *Wall Street Journal* published 240 per day, and BuzzFeed published 222.

My goal was to show just how many online stories happen per day. However, with the wealth of sources and outlets out there, it seems like an almost impossible task.

---

15. Meyer, Robinson, *How Many Stories Do Newspapers Publish Per Day?*, 2016, https://www.theatlantic.com/technology/archive/2016/05/how-many-stories-do-newspapers-publish-per-day/483845/

So, this is only looking at four sources and only their online components. The point here is, the amount of news and opinion that comes out daily is exponential. Add into this the estimated 6,000 to 10,000 ads that PPC Protect claims the average person sees per day,[16] and you'll realize that just to stand out, you need to get through a lot of noise.

So, unless you do something horribly wrong that can get people to watch more news, then the media will not cover your story. That's why its vitally important that you take total responsibility for telling your own story.

It's a twenty-four-hour news cycle, and fear sells.

There are really two lessons to this. The first is that you have to tell your story; no one is looking. The second is that if you're doing big things, eventually someone will complain about you. The second is something I have observed from the clients we have worked with in our PR Firm and also the individuals I have spoken to. Negative press can be a sign you're making an impact. The wrong time to handle bad PR is after it already happens. Gaining media attention and telling your story should be something that you do every single day.

Extraordinary individuals know that to make the biggest possible impact, they have to take total responsibility for getting their message out. They have no problem screaming in from the rooftops because they know it's up to them for others to know who they are and the mission that they serve.

It's also important to know what you are creating when you create attention. As Joe Yazbeck has stated, *"The goal of going on podcasts (or media) is to cultivate enough interest to spark engagement."*

When you get individuals to engage with you, then a conversation can be had about the brand. That engagement is more powerful than

16. Carr, Sam, *How Many Ads Do We See A Day In 2021?*, 2021, https://ppcprotect. com/blog/strategy/how-many-ads-do-we-see-a-day/

any marketing that you can do. It's the power of connection through story that actually gets individuals to buy your brand or product.

You have to be an evangelist, someone willing to shout from the rooftops about your brand and what others need to know about it. It comes down to that "know, like, and trust" factor. Individuals make a choice before they ever meet your brand by what they find online or by what others tell them. So, you have to be the one to fill the void, not let the void be filled by others. When it comes to promoting your own brand, the person I have always thought of is Guy Kawasaki, a man who has become famous for the idea of being an evangelist for a brand.

When it comes down to it, you should be your own best promotion, and as someone who has done it for many brands, including Apple and Canva, Guy knows that he is just the person to tell others about the good works of his own brands. You too need to be the one to tell others what you do, why it is vital to exist in the world, and why they need to be part of it.

## Brand Evangelism: Guy Kawasaki

Guy created the role of Chief Evangelist for Apple, the person who sings from the rooftop all the virtues of their product or service.

Guy grew up in Hawaii in a lower-income family. He went to school on the mainland in California and started out working in the jewelry business before he ended up at the more high-tech end of things at Apple. He was at Apple in the early days, when Steve Jobs was still driving growth.

He ended up in the Macintosh division at Apple, where he was the first software evangelist. He stayed for a while, started his own company, then decided to go back to Apple. Today he's well known for being the brand evangelist for a company from Australia called Canva, which creates online graphic design services.

Guy has also been a Mercedes-Benz Ambassador and a fellow at the Haas School of Business at UC Berkeley.

He is the man credited with coining the term "evangelism" as it relates to business. The word "evangelism" has a bit of a Biblical feel to it—spreading the good news of the Gospel. In the business sense, evangelism relates to telling people about the good news of your company. The word "evangelism" comes from a Greek word, meaning 'bringing the good news.' Guy brought the good news of Macintosh; how it made people more creative and productive. Today, he is bringing the good news of Canva; how it enables people to create great graphics.

Being an evangelist for a company is different from being a salesperson. Typically, the sales orientation is *"I need to make my quota"* or *"I need to make my commission."* Evangelists see things from a different perspective, promoting a product or service because it's good for the customer, not just the company selling it.

So, when using a Macintosh, you are more creative and productive. By using Canva, you have a greater ability to communicate ideas. From that perspective, it's good for the company, but it's also good for you. I can honestly say with both those products, it is good for the customer.

So, what does this look like in implementation? Does the brand evangelist do a lot of speaking? Do they help on the PR side?

First, we must begin with the concept called Guy's Golden Touch: *"Guy's Golden touch is not that whatever I touch turns to gold. Guy's Golden Touch is whatever is gold, Guy touches."*

This is a true depth of belief in the innate goodness of what one is promoting. It is an unshakable confidence in the good of the company.

So what I'm trying to communicate here is that with evangelism, you have to have good news as a starting point. It's very difficult to evangelize crap. So you need to create, or find, or be followed by something great. The rest is easy after that. Really, finding something great is 90 percent of the battle.

Then, you have to take the perspective of why it's good for your customer as opposed to why it's good for you.

## 🎤 Extraordinary Story

**Ethan Beute**: "Creating Stronger Relationships through the Power of Video"

How we communicate has changed drastically. In fact, most of the world has moved to video. As the CEO of Bomb Bomb, a video messaging service, Ethan provides so much value on how to use video to build better relationships and break through the noise.

*www.jeremyryanslate.com/beute*

Let's take a look at an example to really get how the concept works. We'll look at Canva, the online graphic design company.

Canva enables you to create beautiful graphics in minutes. The way in which they do this is through the pre-created templates for all the standard users.

Templates include: social media, book covers, posters, presentations, flyers, all the things that most people have to do. For each of these template types, they've created hundreds of designs. So, you join Canva. You create an account. Then, you pick the type of graphic you want to make. Take Instagram, for example. Canva shows you hundreds of pre-made Instagram designs.

You customize the photo on the text, and you're done. Guy likes to say that you can finish a graphic in Canva faster than you can boot Photoshop. So, this is an example of evangelism that is bringing the good news that now, inexpensively and easily, you can create great graphics you don't need to submit to your graphic design department. You don't have to stand in line. You don't have to pay an independent artist, go through various revisions, and negotiate contracts, and all that.

Canva is empowering you to create your own graphics. Evangelism for a brand is what is good for the customer; it's a given that it's good for the brand, but it puts the needs of the customer first.

## Speak Your Story Fearlessly

It is not just important to communicate your message; it is also important to communicate the right message out to the right people.

For me, there's really been one person who has personally helped me to communicate better in front of a crowd, Joey Yazbeck. I remember meeting Joe at an event back in 2016. I had done a little bit of stage speaking at that point in time. Joe was pulling people up on stage to deliver their message in a short 30-second snippet to the audience to create interest. At that point in time, I didn't really know much about Joe; he just seemed like a very engaging individual that really connected with the audience.

I would later find out he was one of the top speaker coaches on the planet, working with many of the well-known executives out there, in addition to writing a best-selling book himself. He pulled me up on stage to deliver a message and he was impressed at how I had delivered it, but there were a few things he saw that I could change. Over the next few months, I worked with Joe on how I would deliver my message.

Not only was I able to impact people better but I was actually calmer and more relaxed when doing so. How you appear when you deliver your message is vital to actually making an impact. You need to project confidence in your brand. You need to show you know what you're talking about. You need to create trust in those receiving it. So knowing that you are the one to tell your story, it's important to be the right person in that moment to do so.

That calm, cool confidence that speaks for understanding. Not for the ego of the one delivering it. Deliver from calm confidence, not from a shouting delivery.

## Joe Yazbeck: Fearless Public Speaking

The first time Joe got in front of people to speak, he realized it wasn't just about entertaining them and educating them; it was also about uplifting them. He was just six years old, and his parents had brought him to a funeral reception. He didn't quite understand the situation. Everyone was dressed in black and seemed so sad. His mother, noticing that Joe didn't quite understand the situation, said, *"Joey, get up on that table and do that song and dance."*

Confused, Joe looked at his mom and said, *"Why, Mom?"*

She looked back at him and said, *"Because they don't have to be sad."*

It was kind of like an Elvis Presley-type dance. The song was called "Little Darlin" by The Diamonds; kind of a doo-wop-type beat. So, Joe got up on the table, danced and sang, and the whole crowd started clapping. He could notice everyone visibly felt better. In that moment, he made the decision, *"I'm going to do this for the rest of my life."* In fact, Joe thinks by five or six, most people can have an inspiration of what they want to do the rest of their lives, just as he did.

It happened over many years. He involved himself in the entertainment industry. He has a degree in theater. He did a lot of classical theater, even some musical comedy. He still sings professionally to this day. He's had many bands over the years and a production company to help artists in development. He has even helped artists with their stage presence as well as their delivery of their promotion and marketing.

## Extraordinary Fact

Demosthenes lived in Athens from 384 BCE to 322 BCE. As a young man, he suffered from a speech impediment—which may have been a stutter, an inability to pronounce the "r" sound, or both. He designed a series of exercises for himself to improve his speech.

According to legend, he practiced speaking with stones in his mouth, which forced him to work very hard to get the sounds out. When his diction became clearer, he got rid of the stones and found he was able to enunciate much more effectively than before.[17]

Mastering public speaking is one of the most important skills. Though this may be something you fear or dread, at least you won't have to put stones in your mouth!

For Joe, it was in his family. His father was a musician. His son is a major Broadway star in New York. In fact, his son does concerts all over the United States and is also a leading man on Broadway. It's in Joe's blood.

When you are able to stand up on stage and be yourself and effect change on an audience, it's an incredible thing. It is something Joe not only learned from his experience, but he took it and wrote his book to help others to do the same where they can. Any leader of a company, any executive, any community-organizing leader, or any public servant can learn these tools and learn how to motivate an audience to a call to action to create positive change.

One of the major things I've noticed about Joe and much of his written and spoken work is this immense desire to lead people with the spoken word.

17. Kissell, Joe, *Demosthenes' Stones*, 2018, https://itotd.com/articles/4074/demosthenes-stones/

He had initially done a lot of consulting with companies and had a realization: owners and executives of companies were actually very poor communicators. It was for this reason that management could not coordinate well. To really win and grow a company, it takes communication and coordination amongst their teams. To really put a project together requires project coordination, and if they weren't coordinating at all, what were they really doing?

It was at that moment that Joe realized that stage presence for public speaking was not about just performing artists or those people who were looking to be on camera. Rather, it was for board meetings, negotiating, sales presentations, and hiring. All these things required communication for impact and were essential to running an effective company.

Joe then decided that he would transition not into public speaking but into leadership quality communications. The term "public speaking," for a lot of people, brings with it jitters; for others, excitement. For many people, the thought of public speaking is one of the scariest things. So, Joe decided to take this new direction and teach leaders how to speak. When a leader can learn how to speak, they become respected and then they can really run a successful organization.

## 🎤 Extraordinary Story

**Michael Port**: "Unleashing the Heroic Public Speaker Within"

Michael Port is one of the most famous public speakers in the world. He's confident that anyone can learn to deliver to an audience. What I learned from him in this conversation changed my outlook.

*www.jeremyryanslate.com/port*

It has a lot to do with confidence building to be able to speak charismatically. Then you can inspire an audience for your team. That's what leadership should be doing.

They should understand the tools and competencies of leadership, which is what Joe's company provides. He calls them *"core competencies."* At the same time, Joe's company is about unleashing champions. How do you unleash? If you look at people, typically, when you hear them speak, they're restrained, they're constrained, they're withdrawn.

They're reciting their presentations by memory. Which makes them completely boring.

I remember seeing John C. Maxwell speak and seeing Joe speak. He had that same vibe around him. Comfortable, just like they were speaking to a friend.

However, for most major events I've went to over the last 10 years, that does not seem to be the case. Speakers are yelling, they're amped up, they're jumping. In actuality, they're not comfortable being there at all. For the seasoned veteran, it's actually quite obvious. Just as Joe Yazbeck and John C Maxwell do, it's the individual that can comfortably be there, communicate, and make the audience leave changed that really communicates, not the one yelling at them, to amp them up.

## Authenticity and Being Comfortable as a Speaker

When we look at the authenticity of a speaker, where does that really come from? It's not about borrowing someone else's personality to become more powerful. It's not about developing yourself to become someone different. In fact, Joe says he doesn't care if *"you're four foot seven, three hundred pounds, have a wart on your nose and Coke-bottle glasses. You can be as charismatic as anyone else."* It just comes down to getting rid of what doesn't belong, the things that shouldn't be there as a speaker. Every single individual has qualities you want to have show up. Those qualities are the inherent traits that make that individual authentic.

It's a very interesting experience. As an audience member it makes you more comfortable if you can perceive that the one speaking to you from the stage is comfortable. This is what Joe calls the 5 C's of a commanding speaker.

One of those five C's is comfort. Comfortability. Are you okay? There's caring, there's confidence, there's credibility, and then there's comfortability. A speaker who's comfortable with others is also charismatic. Comfortability is putting your audience at ease and making them feel they're in a conversation with you, one on one; that's the key to it.

You have to be comfortable in your own skin. That's where the term "*stage presence*" comes from.

The key to stage presence is: "*How present are you?*" Further, it is: "*To what degree are you there?*" You have to show up, but you have to show up fully. You cannot show up if you're thinking, because that's looking inward. If you're standing up in front of a camera or in front of an audience, and you're thinking of what to say, people hate it and it feels scripted. They hate it. When you've got a teleprompter, they know you're reading it.

The key is to be as open, comfortable, confident, intentful, and intentional as you can be about what you want to say.

Going back to those speakers that feel the need to pump you up from stage—they're masking something. They're not comfortable. So they're hyping it. Joe isn't one for hype, which he finds akin to ranting. He remembers speaks like Wayne Dyer, who was very good at relaxing and being comfortable and just talking to his audience and giving examples. He wasn't into hype. Audiences loved him for that.

A speaker that can deliver like Dyer did makes the audience feel more significant. To that effect, Joe recalls he had an opportunity to train the chief technology officer of Hewlett Packard worldwide.

He's the top tech guy for HP, and he and Joe are still great friends today. In fact, Joe says that's what he loves about his business: he gets to be best friends with incredible powerhouses. This chief technology officer was an introvert. He was an algorithmic, linear-thinking guy; a genius at building things.

This man realized the importance of real life. He had built this video conferencing setup for the meetings he would have. He created these virtual video conference rooms where he would bring people in to have their meetings. He put a lot of attention into making people comfortable. He would bring things into the room specifically for the people he was going to converse with: knowledge of their favorite foods, where they liked to travel, how many kids they had and their ages. So, he would have these incredible conversations with these people, and the business meeting had not even started yet. It was a masterful example of creating comfortability in the environment to have stronger communication.

This is what heightened the affinity or the likeability factor before they got into solving problems with project coordination. It made a huge difference; they were actually talking to each other.

## Putting Together a Winning Talk

So, we've looked at what it takes to actually be there and communicate. However, when we look at putting together a winning talk, one that actually impacts, what does that look like? I posed that very question to Joe Yazbeck. The answer started with getting their attention right out of the starting gate. The speaker should pose a problem that the audience are challenged with, right at the beginning of their communication.

The speaker should want to have the audience look at something that they're having a hard time looking at; that is a challenge in itself. Then, the speaker should construct a rhetorical question or a series of questions that gets them to look at the problems they're challenged with, rather than talk about himself or herself. Rather than talk about their own business and who they are, forget all that; focus on the problem of the audience.

Get their attention by throwing a dart at them or punching them with an impinging impact to get attention. For example, from the field of speaking, Joe may ask an executive: *"Are you an executive that is restraining yourself from getting out in front of people on stage or on camera because you risk the chance of being embarrassed or humiliated?"*

Joe continues:

> *"I can ask two or three other types of questions like that. Are you risking giving staff meetings because you're afraid or nervous in front of your own peers and you don't want to reduce your reputation or credibility? If the answer is yes, you'd better take a look at..."*

A setup to talk such as this gets you up and running. Now, instead of speaking at the audience, you're really in communication with what they need to hear and how they need to hear it. Then, you're off and running.

Now, the audience is able to take a look at your message. Next, you want to give them a sense of how they've been affected by that problem. What that does is help the audience to get a sense that you know what they need to know, and that you care about them. The care factor is vital to actually communicating with the audience.

You take them through that step of, *"I can understand your frustration; here's what happens."* So then, the next step is key to real impact. You have to show them what the consequences are if they do nothing. The audience needs to be shown some examples of the ripple effect, if they do nothing about it, and what would happen. Basically, you're making them aware of how things get worse if they do nothing. Nothing in this world ever stays the same, and you have to show them that. That is a turning point for most people.

So in presentations, in the one- to two-minute tip, a speaker can bring up what would happen if an audience member did nothing. Joe says, *"You see how much money you are leaving on the table."* He continues, *"In other words, give them a sense of a bucket with a hole in the bottom where you keep pouring money in it."*

Now that they have truly grasped how dire the situation is, the speaker has to show them what can be done about it. That's where you commit to giving them the benefits of doing something or give them the benefits of coming to talk to you about what you can do about it.

Don't tell them how; just give them a reason to come see you. That's when you close with a call to action; leading your audience to you as a solution.

## Extraordinary Takeaways

I have dedicated my life to the idea of telling my own story and the stories of others. I've learned from experience that no one is going to tell your story for you. That's exactly why I founded my company, Command Your Brand. We help leaders to tell their stories through the power of appearing as a guest on top-rated podcasts. If you're a leader and you're looking for help with that, then check us out www.commandyourbrand.com.

It's sad that not more people realize that you have to be the one to tell your story. It's almost like a weird thing we're taught when we are raised. We're told "don't boast," or "stop bragging." These are things we were told as kids, and we can't seem to drop them for the rest of our lives, even if these tendencies are counterproductive. As we've seen here, whether it's through a brand evangelist, like Guy Kawasaki, or through learning how to speak better, as we learn through Joe Yazbeck, you have to get out there and get in front of the people and tell them the good works about what you do.

When you look at it, to live is to communicate. If you're not communicating, then you're not living, and if you're not living, then there's no way you're going to grow. To be extraordinary is to understand that you're not boasting; you're doing what you need to do to survive— telling your story.

Become responsible for your story, get good at telling it, and tell it to all the people who matter. I'm reminded of a story of Alexander the Great. At 18 years old, he led his father's army for the first time, and before the age of 30, he conquered the known world. Here's the interesting part about it: he didn't wait for others to tell his story. In fact, he brought his own publicist with him. His scribe, Arrian, accompanied him on all his campaigns. Arrian then wrote a book about the entire career of Alexander. Of course, Alexander approved the copy first; he was paying for it.

Those that tell you not to promote your own achievements are afraid of what you may achieve. Don't listen to them. Tell your own story, because no one else is going to do it for you.

# 10. Radical Responsibility

*The man who complains about the way the ball*
*bounces is likely to be the one who dropped it.*

— Lou Holtz

The path to success isn't what you think, and you don't get there how you think you do.

The scariest thing is when you discover that you are fully responsible for your life, but on the flip side of that, it's also the most empowering thing that can happen to you.

It's crazy to me that most people go through life like a ping pong ball. *"Look what this person did to me,"* ping. *"Look what happened to me,"* pong. *"I just need something good to happen to me,"* ping. *"Someone needs to give me an opportunity,"* pong.

This type of thinking is no-responsibility thinking, but it's how most of the world gets through life. Most people believe someone else is to blame for their situation and won't take a good look in the mirror to find the person who is actually responsible.

The hardest thing in life is to take responsibility for what you did or even what you failed to do because when you do that, you have to admit fault. Most people just can't do that.

To be truly extraordinary, one realizes that they can change situations. If you created a bad one, then then the good news is that you can create a good one.

I see this as the biggest reason that most people will never be extraordinary. They want to make someone else responsible for their life. Their economic situation is someone else's fault. Their political situation is someone else's fault. Why they haven't advanced at their job is someone else's fault. However, once you can get past that blaming and truly look at your own responsibilities, it's actually very interesting. You can even see it in how you communicate. For example, when someone blows up on you, you ask yourself: What did you do to cause that? If you were to ask most people this question, n they would totally blame it on the other person, but most likely, they had some sort of a part to play in what they just experienced.

When you learn to take broader responsibility for your life, the things that happened to you in it, and for your part in every conversation, you'll see a lot of positive things start to happen in your life.

To be extraordinary, one must understand that life comes down to them, and then have the courage to act on that. However, it's not that many lack the knowledge, but that they lack the will.

To me the best example of this is auto racing. Drivers go at a high rate of speed. One mistake is quite deadly. A car can swerve, wreck, and take out a bunch of others. It's the easiest and most visible example of total responsibility. It has plenty of applications in life—that one step out of line can lead to broader effects, and can wreck your life, to put it simply.

Open-wheel racing, the cars that drive in the Indianapolis 500 every year, is one of the fastest forms of racing on the planet. Cars go down a straightaway into a high banked turn, going 220 miles an hour. They don't have time to blame someone else; they have to observe and react—more accurately, do both almost at the exact same time. There's no room for mistakes. Mistakes lead to injury and sometimes death.

## Extraordinary Fact

Over the decades, the number of deaths has reduced even as the number of Formula 1 races has increased.

While 18 drivers died in the first decade of Formula 1 racing, ending in 1960, 14 died in the following decade. The number of deaths dropped to 10 in the decade leading up to 1980.

From 1982 to 1994, five drivers died, culminating with the death of Roland Ratzenberger and Ayrton Senna on successive days. A further five drivers died after that till 2017 with Jules Bianchi being the only fatality in a Championship race.

Fifty-two Formula One drivers have died to date, either while testing, practicing, qualifying, or racing in Formula One.[18]

I had a conversation with Helio Castroneves, at the time of my conversation, a three-time Indy 500 Champion, now, a four-time Indy 500 champion. The Indianapolis 500 is one of the most storied events in all in of Motorsports. It's not just another race. There's more pageantry, excitement, and a higher level of difficulty. It's like the Super Bowl of motorsports.

Helio Castroneves has never won an IndyCar title. However, he's won what some claim to be the most storied race in all of

---

18. Partridge, Jarrod, *Deaths in Formula 1*, 2020, https://f1chronicle.com/deaths-in-formula-1/

motorsports, the Daytona 500, an incredible four times. I find that more impressive than winning a championship.

In baseball, they call the situation when the game is on the line a high-leverage situation. It is the highest possible stress that one can be under. Players like Jonathan Loaisiga, Pete Fairbanks, and Craig Kimbrel thrive in these situations. They come in to get 1 to 3 outs, throw 10 to 30 pitches at nearly one hundred miles per hour, and their night is done.

To put this into perspective, the Indianapolis 500 is like five hundred miles of high-leverage situations. It's like coming in with the bases loaded and a full count on the batter and you can't make a mistake. Drivers operate in that environment for three or four hours.

To me, it is the ultimate in stress, and to win in that situation, four times at that, is a very impressive achievement.

## Helio Castroneves, Four-Time Indianapolis 500 Winner

Helio Castroneves was born in Sao Paulo, Brazil, and had an interest in racing from a very young age. His father used to love race cars. He was a used car salesman and always watched TV racing, especially Formula One.

Helio fondly remembers fondly watching those races with his father, playing with his Matchbox cars, running around on an imaginary racetrack. His father got involved in putting together a stock car team in Brazil and ended up building a team for a few races. He had his own company, and he basically started using the car as a marketing tool to promote the company. He threw the company's branding and logo on it so that people would see his company going around the track. His father would bring Helio to work with him, let him sit behind the steering wheel and do some imaginary driving. Proof positive of the power of dreams.

In the middle of that season, one of the members of the team could see how much love Helio had for racing. So, he bought him a small go-kart. Helio raced that little go-kart all around the neighborhood. Until one day his dad bought him a realgo-kart, a very exciting gift.

1987 was the first year his father entered the championships in San Paulo. Helio was a small-town kid getting a chance to go to the big city. It was a bit intimidating, but he started making a lot of friends. He looks at that as the time when he actually fell in love with racing. It wasn't just about racing; it was actually about community. It felt like a huge neighborhood, away from his home neighborhood. It was some place where he would always feel at home, no matter where it was.

For him, it was really cool to have that kind of education, understanding, and way of growing up. Seeing that he had such a small-time start, it was interesting for me to learn how he went from that small-town kid from San Paulo to one of the top racers in the world.

He compares racing early on to different levels in school. You know you're actually improving when you're getting wins and getting good results. So, when you're winning enough times, you make the decision to advance to the next level or get invited to do so. In 1994, he completed his final season at F3 South America. From there, in 1995, he moved to England so that he could race in the British Formula 3.

It was an interesting experience for a young Helio. He finished third in the championship that year, right behind his two teammates. He had a meeting with his sponsors, and they informed him that they wanted to start a Brazilian team racing in America. With the success he had just had in Europe, Helio was not really planning on leaving and informed his sponsors of this. They let him know were he to make the decision not to move to America, then their sponsorship relationship in Europe was over. So, with no choice but to go, he left for America in 1996.

## 🎤 Extraordinary Story

**Danica Patrick**: "The Racer's Mindset Transformed to Business and Life"

Auto racing has long been perceived as a male driven sport. Though other women have competed in the past, Danica Patrick has been the first to bring it week after week. More than that, she has managed to build a highly visible media brand. That visibility has helped to show other females there can be a place for them in motorsports.

*www.jeremyryanslate.com/danica*

---

In 1998, he came to IndyCar. It was there that he found that same love as that boy driving go karts in Sao Paulo. I remember myself, sitting with my dad, watching him in 2001 win his first Indianapolis 500. It was that day when Helio Castroneves became my favorite IndyCar driver.

## As a Four-Time Indianapolis Winner

When I first spoke to Helio, he was a three-time Indianapolis 500 winner. In May 2021, he became a four-time winner of the race. With that feat, Helio became one of only four drivers—Rick Mears, AJ Foyt, Al Unser, and himself—to win the race four times.

The Indianapolis 500 is the big spectacle in racing, the biggest race in the world, the toughest racing that you can possibly imagine because it's three hours.

The pure sprint tradition is incredible. And it's been around for over one hundred years. Indianapolis is a place where a car can hit over 230 miles an hour.

Helio says of the track, "The place is it's magic." It's a place where having the best car and the best driver may not matter. Castroneves is well aware that the race is about being in the right place at the right time, and that's how he has done it four times. When talking about winning the race on multiple occasions, he claims winning once isn't hard but following up may be the single most difficult thing to do, especially three more times.

To put it in perspective, when Castroneves won the race again in 2002, it was the first time in over 30 years that a driver had won the race back to back since Al Unser Sr.

## Extraordinary Fact

The most Indianapolis 500 wins by a driver is four, achieved by AJ Foyt (USA) in 1961, 1964, 1967 and 1977; Al Unser Sr (USA) in 1970–71, 1978 and 1987; Rick Mears (USA) in 1979, 1984, 1988 and 1991; and Hélio Castroneves (Brazil) in 2001–02, 2009 and 2021.

The first run occurred May 30, 1911. The Indianapolis 500 is a 500-mile (804-km) automobile race around 200 laps of the Indianapolis Motor Speedway in Indiana, USA. Castroneves won a record-equaling fourth race on May 30, 2021 at the age of 46. His average speed was 190.690 mph (306.885 km/h), the fastest ever recorded.[19]

When he heard the doubters, Helio was confident in his skills, believing he was a driver with talent above the others. He did not just show up to compete; he showed up to win. This is what made him decide that it is the track that picks you. He was close to going a lap down; the car setup had been really tough. The team had spent a month there preparing, but somehow, they had missed the setup.

---

19. Guinness Book of World Records Editor, *Most Indianapolis 500 Wins*, 2021, https://www.guinnessworldrecords.com/world-records/most-indianapolis-500-wins/

However, they found their opportunity in strategy. With the laps winding down, all the teams, except Helio's, elected to make pit stops. At the time, he was running in 15th place, and the team decided to gamble, thinking anything had to be better than 15th. That decision left him leading the race. They cut it close on fuel, but with only two laps to go, a caution flag came out, and he knew at that point he would win the race; second year in a row.

Second year in a row. Unbelievable.

## The Single Hardest Year with a Win

2009 was the single hardest year of Helio's racing career. He was embroiled in a court case with the IRS, who claimed he owed thousands of dollars in back taxes. He would later come out the victor, over the IRS, but in May of that year, during the Indianapolis 500, he was still deeply embroiled in the legal battle.

Helio attributes winning the race for a third time to loving what he does each and every day. Racing for him is an environment where his problems drift away. The only thing there becomes him and the car. I think when you look at extraordinary individuals, that's something they all have in common: the ability to block out all the noise and just do what they're good at.

He claims that for him, racing is like therapy; he can't actually think of anything other than racing while in the car. To do anything else would be unsafe for himself and for other drivers. Helios says, *"So you take your mind away from all of the problems, all of the issues, you don't think about, wives, kids, girlfriends or money problems or whatever."*

Doing anything other than driving takes too much energy. It makes sense when you think about it. He's getting into action, one of the best things you can do when things get tough. A driver has to be focused. Your mind is so consumed with the information that the car is giving you: the track, the weather, etc. There are just some things that a driver can perceive that cannot be translated to an engineer, no matter how you explain it. Therefore, a driver can only focus on the track.

Helio says it was the perfect scenario for him. 2009 was a very difficult year, but being back in an environment he knew very well helped him to block out the noise. He believes that is the biggest reason he won the 2009 Indianapolis 500.

### Separation from Fear

Auto racing NASCAR or IndyCar is one of the most dangerous sports on the planet. I remember many races I watched as a spectator that a driver did not walk away from. In 2001 I was watching the Daytona 500 when my father's favorite driver, Dale Earnhardt, crashed into the Turn 4 wall after a battle with Sterling Marlin on the final lap and lost his life.

After Earnhardt's wreck, NASCAR invested greatly in driver safety. they added head and neck restraints and created softer barriers in an effort to protect drivers. For a sport that had frequently lost drivers, Dale Earnhardt was the last NASCAR driver to pass away in a race more than 20 years ago. This was proof positive in the 2020 Daytona 500, when driver Ryan Newman experienced one of the worst crashes I have ever seen and lived to tell about it.

## Extraordinary Story

**Kelley Earnhardt-Miller**: "The 9 Lessons that Changed this NASCAR Legend's Life"

When preparing to speak to Kelley, I heard her state in an interview that she did not like being asked about being a woman in motorsports; I did not ask her that question. Though carrying the name of her famous father, Dale Earnhardt, Kelley has built a name for herself as one of the most powerful executives in motorsports.

*www.jeremyryanslate.com/earnhardt*

---

NASCAR or stock car racing and IndyCar or open-wheel racing are two very different types of motorsports. In a stock car, the driver is completely covered by the shell of the car, and it is rare for a car to ever exceed 200 miles an hour. In an open-wheel car, the driver's upper body and head are exposed, and cars can go over 230 miles an hour. Open-wheel racing is a very different type of risk than stock car racing.

In 2011, I was sitting and watching the Indianapolis 500 with my father as I usually do. A horrible wreck took the life of former Indianapolis 500 winner, Dan Wheldon. For me personally, driver safety was something very important to talk to Helio about. I wanted to know how he balanced the danger of the sport with the risks he needed to take to win. How does one separate the two?

When the driver plays it safe, he may not take the risks he needs to win a race. Whereas if the driver takes too many risks, he may be putting himself in a life-threatening position or he could become seriously injured.

His response is something I believe is very applicable for all of us:

> "It's just fear. You've got to learn how to deal with that. I know every human being has fear, feelings of fear, and you've just got to block that in a normal way. Some people make it a little harder. So now, in our sport, you've just got to be able to see that we understand the dangers of it. We know the risks of it, but at the same time, we love it. If you were to tell me to do something else, I probably wouldn't be happy.

*And that's a very strange thing to say, but that's what I love to do. It's a shame that we lost a lot of colleagues during my career. Those unfortunately lost is where we were able to improve safety so that doesn't happen again, but it's still it's a dangerous sport."*

Fear will always be there. It's those of us who can block it out and push forward that will become extraordinary.

## Extraordinary Takeaway

Motorsports are the most extreme example of radical responsibility. However, when you look at it, many of us are dealing with life and death every single day. If you don't stop at that stop sign, you could cause a car accident. If you don't take all the proper precautions, then someone else could get hurt. If you don't pay your taxes, you could go to jail.

Many of the things we complain about most often come down to responsibility. How responsible are you willing to be for your own life? This can be one of the hardest things to train into ourselves because we're always told that someone else is responsible for us. The more responsible you are, the freer are you are. The less responsible you are, the more you fall under the control of another. That's how modern slavery happens. When you look at it, we fall under the control of social media companies because it's easy. We fall under the control of Amazon because it's easy. We let politicians run our lives because it's easy.

The responsible thing and the easy thing are usually the exact opposite. The thing I want you to walk away from this chapter with is you have some level of responsibility for every single thing in your life. If you have a bad relationship, then what could you have done differently to change that relationship? If you're not advancing in your job, then what could you do in that job? You could even go as far as getting a new job. I've been there. I've blamed the opportunity, not my own ability to make the opportunity work for me.

Responsibility is that scary thing that can make us all extraordinary. However, because many never want to really be responsible, they will never be extraordinary. So, even if you start with small things, you'll have a leg up on most of the world. Being more responsible for your own life, income, and your family's safety will be a game changer.

Once you start figuring out how you can be more responsible and stop blaming others, and stop playing the victim, then you can start to create an extraordinary life.

# 11. The Duty of Leadership

*Leadership is something you earn, something you're chosen for. You can't come in yelling, "I'm your leader!" If it happens, it's because the other guys respect you.*

— Ben Roethlisberger

Extraordinary people have a greater understanding of leadership. The ordinary person will just comfortably go through life, doing things that don't hurt too much. Extraordinary people are willing to go through the inconvenience and the pain to achieve greatness.

Extraordinary people realize that there are two types of people in the masses: the sheep that will just be led to the slaughter and continue to go; and the sheepdogs, those responsible for organizing the packs of others and those who take responsibility for the actions of others. They're the ones that protect democracy, the freedoms of others, and put a future there for other people to live in. Where the artist sees the future, the sheepdogs ensure the future is still there.

The craziness of the past two years has led me to realize that myself and other people I see as extraordinary are the sheepdogs.

We're not willing to put up with a loss of freedom, a hindrance on our thinking, and we see it is our responsibility to protect others.

Personally, I found inspiration in a lot of military leaders. I've read *American Soldier* by General Tommy Franks, poured over thousands of pages of books by Tom Clancy, and been inspired by learning of the courage of General U.S. Grant in the Civil War. Other than committing yourself to a religious life, the military is one of the biggest commitments to service that you can make.

The great generals of old have been something of interest to me: Washington, Paton, MacArthur, and Eisenhower. Our modern military carries on a long heritage of leadership. Frankly, when many people think of the military, I believe one of the first things that come to mind for them is leadership.

As someone who did not serve, I have been very motivated to find out what makes military leadership so different.

In this chapter, I will focus on a conversation I had with one of the most decorated military leaders of our time: Four-Star General David H. Petraeus. It was a bit shocking to me that we actually connected for a conversation, even though we'd been connected on LinkedIn for some time. How that started, I'm not sure. Most likely, I'm the one that requested his connection. However, we have consistently engaged on each other's posts.

One day, I sent the general a message, asking if I could do a podcast interview with him. He responded that he'd love to, but I would have to follow up with him in a year. Being that I'm not like most, I keep a long-running spreadsheet for the people I want to follow up with for interviews. So, nearly one year to the day, I followed up with General Petraeus. His calendar had opened up, but he had asked to see exactly what I wanted to talk about before we spoke. To me this seemed like a test. I needed to show the general that speaking to me would be the best use of his time.

I did not want to mess this up so I reached out to connections to ask the best questions of General Petraeus. I reached out to a few people I knew that had actually worked with him, one being Major General Gregg Sturdevant. Major General Sturtevant and I exchanged emails for a few days before I came up with six questions that I wanted to ask General Petraeus. I wrote them up neatly and responded to his message. He accepted the interview. What follows is my greatest learnings of military leadership and what it means at its highest levels.

## General David Petraeus

General David Petraeus is a retired Four-Star United States Army General and public official. He served as Director of the Central Intelligence Agency from September 6, 2011, until his resignation on November 9, 2012.

Prior to his assuming the directorship of the CIA, Petraeus served 37 years in the United States Army. His last assignments in the Army were as commander of the International Security Assistance Force (ISAF) and Commander, U.S. Forces – Afghanistan (USFOR-A) from July 4, 2010 to July 18, 2011.

His other four-star assignments include serving as the 10th Commander, U.S. Central Command (USCENTCOM) from October 13, 2008 to June 30, 2010, and as Commanding General, Multi-National Force – Iraq (MNF-I) from February 10, 2007 to September 16, 2008. As commander of MNF-I, Petraeus oversaw all coalition forces in Iraq.

The biggest thing that I wondered about General Petraeus is why he chose to commit his career to the service of his country. He not only attended West Point, but upon retiring continued to serve his country as the head of the Central Intelligence Agency. What motivated such a commitment?

Well, as one gets into a career in uniform, one discovers certain elements, and if one enjoys those, if one feels challenged by them, if one has opportunities that are fulfilling, if one has chances to go between different activities, as Petraeus was privileged to do, say as an infantry company commander, then one feels inspired to continue his service. One day, under a rucksack, literally, and Kevlar helmet, and then going to graduate school at Princeton a couple of years later, teaching at West point, then back to a unit in the great 101st airborne division and so forth.

So, back and forth between positions that call for real physical stamina and ability for real, enormous leadership opportunities at a fairly young age, or leading a platoon as a second Lieutenant of some 43 or 44 paratroopers in Vicenza, Italy, as an example, as Petraeus was privileged to do. For him, the motivation lay just the whole notion of performing a mission that is larger than itself.

## 🎙 Extraordinary Story

**Maj. Gen. Gregg Sturdevant**: "Leadership, Legacy and Solutions when the Mission is Critical"

Major General Gregg Sturdevant has led some of the Marine Corps' most difficult battles. In this episode we discuss how to weigh a decision from a military viewpoint and how it applies to life and the corporate world.

*www.jeremyryanslate.com/sturdevant*

Petraeus is thankful just to have the extraordinary privilege, the opportunity, to serve with fellow Americans, particularly in the wake of the 9/11 attacks and in the wars of the post 9/11 period, where

Americans have raised their right hands and taken an oath to serve in uniform, knowing that they're going to deploy to combat and likely going to do it again. And in some cases, deployment again and again after that.

So, for Petraeus, it was really, something that was beyond special. To him, there is no greater privilege than that kind of service and service with others who feel the same way and at a time when Americans, even if they disagreed with the policies we were implementing, at least supported our young men and women in uniform and their families.

At the end of Petraeus' time in uniform, President Obama gave him the opportunity to continue to serve his country. To stay, in a sense, in the fight against those who had brought 9/11 to us back in 2001. He sees that still as an extraordinary privilege and opportunity.

To me that seems like the real difference. Petraeus repeatedly referred to his service as a privilege and an honor. I don't believe there are many people who see what they do is a privilege and an honor. To carry oneself that way and to lead in that way really is different from most areas of life. I think this viewpoint is one of the major things that makes military leadership different. In a world where most people are annoyed at the idea of having to take responsibility, our military see service and responsibility to our country as a privilege and honor. If more of us could approach our work as a privilege and an honor, I think we could find greatness in that.

## Writing as a Way of Honing Thoughts

Writing, as someone famously observed, helps you distill your thoughts. It forces you actually to distill the ideas.

It's an action-forcing mechanism. The commitment to write as Petraeus did with the Counterinsurgency Field Manual—and to publish that in less than a year during the time that he was back in the United States between his three- and four-star tours in Iraq—for example, was a huge intellectual journey for himself and all of those who were engaged in it.

It provided the intellectual foundation on which they built the strategy, the big ideas of the surge, which were a near-180-degree shift from what they'd been doing before. Writing, even if it was an article about physical training, just tended to force him to sit down and to truly lay out his own thinking and to do it as obviously, as coherently, as concisely and effectively he possibly could.

It's often been that Petreaus gets an idea while running or in the shower or in another situation like that, and then idea seems crystal clear at that time. I think we can all relate to this. Then, when you try to write it down and to lay it out and to develop it, it actually turns out that it wasn't quite so crystal clear. It's the action of trying to lay that out in writing that forces you to do that.

General Petraeus is a big believer in what could be termed action-forcing mechanisms. Meaning, there's nothing as productive as setting a deadline for yourself and committing to it publicly to others, whether it is that you're going to run a marathon in two hours and 50 minutes, or you're going to do a PhD and have all the work done except for the dissertation itself.

It's these kinds of exercises that General Petraeus has found very, very meaningful. They forced him to sit down and to, as clearly as he could, lay out the various ideas that he had on various issues. It still is the case. He'll occasionally commit to an op-ed piece, for the *Wall Street Journal* or the *Washington Post* on what America should have learned from the last 20 years of war against Islamist extremists or related issues.

It's a very intellectually challenging and often fulfilling endeavor. It forces you to look at things a different way and figure out, do these narratives fit together? Do these ideas fit together?

It makes us question our thinking. I think writing definitely makes us work out a lot of our ideas before we put them into the real world. It also provides you intellectual capital, which you can draw from later. General Petraeus is also a believer that a senior thesis or monograph, a dissertation, whatever it is that we end up producing over the years should ideally be on topics that do provide intellectual capital for the future.

When Petraeus did his dissertation on the American military and the lessons of Vietnam, it was a tremendously instructive project for him. People might think that these large writing projects are overrated, but they certainly are significant for the person doing the research, and the writing, and the analysis. Years later, Petraeus reflected back on his own thesis when all of a sudden, he was the individual providing advice on the use of force.

Situations and examples and historical cases that he had examined in the post-Vietnam era when force was considered colored his advice and how it was provided. It was very, very helpful. Many years later, it was even helpful when he was the executive officer for the Chairman of the Joint Chiefs of Staff for two years when he was a colonel.

He distinctly remembers walking in and saying:

> *"You know, boss, historically, no president has ever decided to use force if a Chairman of the Joint Chiefs opposed it. So just think about the significance of what it is that your advice holds in one of these meetings and the situation room at the West Wing of the White House."*

All from work he had done many years before. Writing can be such a powerful experience for intellectual growth.

## How a Leader Carries Himself

General Petraeus believes that your leadership style shouldn't be something that's fixed and inviolate. It actually should be whatever is required to bring out the best in each individual you lead. You're privileged to lead individually. In other words, your direct reports, each of them, will be different for each individual.

Some might need a pat on the back once a year. Others might need it once an hour. Still others might need an application of a boot to some part of their anatomy. In addition, obviously, the more senior a person gets, the more he might have an inflated ego for you to deal with. Sometimes, the more special people think they are, the more delicate you have to be in dealing with them.

### 🎙 Extraordinary Story

**Jim Tressel**: "The Philosophy of Ohio State's Football National Champion Coach"

After my interview with AJ Hawk, I was struck by what he learned as a college football player about how to be a better man, not just an athlete. That led me to reach out to Jim Tressel, a coach that led Ohio State football to an undefeated and national championship season.

*www.jeremyryanslate.com/tressel*

When one gets to very senior ranks, obviously you're dealing with people who have been very successful, but you still have to lead them. It's not a case of imposing your will on them. It's a case of persuading them, convincing them, getting them to support wholeheartedly and willingly and to contribute.

If that person thinks that you're off base, then you need to explain your rationale for decisions. Then obviously, in coalition leadership, there is a whole new batch of folks who are very sensitive about national identities and anything that could be interpreted as criticism. In Petraeus' case, he had to deal with nation parners, such as the Prime Minister of Iraq, or the President of Afghanistan, not to mention our own political leaders, who are not without egos either.

Each individual is so different. That's why it's so important to understand the personality traits, the strengths, the weaknesses, the susceptibility to flatter, all of these different elements that make up a person's identity.

Petraeus says he would try to be a person of small ego but wasn't always successful. He also says that if you are at very senior levels and you do encounter a degree of success, then it becomes harder to suppress that. He recalls how fortunate he was, to work for a boss, early on when he was still with two-star General, Major General Jack Galvin, as a captain. He was Galvin's aide when he was in division commander.

Galvin was really quite famous for being understated and being low maintenance, as Petraeus puts it. He would really try to have his aide focus on the substantive aspects of the job, rather than bringing over a perfectly mixed martini with one or two olives or something like that in the blink of an eye.

He said to Petraeus:

> *"Look, just send the waiter over to me. I'll get a drink, don't worry. You sort out what's going on and talk to your fellow aides and figure out what's happening behind the scenes. Figure out what's going on in the units that you and I haven't actually laid eyes on."*

He wanted Petraeus to expand his impact, not to be his cigarette lighter. He worked for him twice more. In fact, when he was a four-star general, culminating with him being the NATO Supreme Allied Commander, Europe, he still had a very small ego. He did things that Petraeus actually couldn't bring himself to do.

He would wear only two rows of ribbons, whereas Petraeus let his continue to expand as he got them, at least to the point where he ran out of room. Galvin was a man of a tremendous modesty; he was on receive, not on transmit.

Galvin was a very admirable example; he was also a soldier's scholar and had written three books. By the time Petraeus worked for him, he wrote one more. Petraeus helped with the final book that Galvin wrote. In fact, Petraeus delivered the eulogy at his funeral at Arlington cemetery; he was a statesman as well.

There are certainly many others who had various attributes and strengths and capabilities that you can also try to develop in yourself, but Petraeus sees the army as somewhat unique because one has to have this mix of need for a fairly substantial physical dimension, especially in the infantry, but also warfare is a technical field. One really does have to understand how to use all these different weapons systems and fuse types and how to orchestrate complex tactics.

It is a profession for those who have a special body of knowledge in a professional ethos, and you spend years and years and years, decades trying to master that profession, in the hope that should there be a need to employ those capabilities, you are ready to do that.

Most go through their careers and don't have that opportunity, even though they may be ready, but it just doesn't come. Though it's not that they're wishing for it. Petraeus really doesn't believe that the military wants to have wars in order to demonstrate their abilities.

Those who have seen war and know the real cost and sacrifice that is entailed in combat are not keen to see this either continue or expand or embark on new wars. However, Petraeus also recognizes that the way to prevent war, to deter conflict, is obviously to be capable of it.

## Strategic Leadership and Courage

Now that Petraeus has been in the private sector for a little over seven years, most recently as a partner in global investment firm KKR, he has had a chance to experience some civilian leadership. The ones on whom he focuses the most are those that exercise strategic leadership. These are the individuals who founded a company or are leading a company at a very high level, or, as in the case of Jeff Bezos, have literally built the entire company and continue to lead it.

## Extraordinary Story

**Robin Sharma**: "The Essential Elements to Creating Leadership in Yourself"

Robin Sharma has worked with some of the most influential people in the world, world-class athletes, and even United States Presidents. He has a vast insight into leadership, the most important of which is that you must first lead yourself to lead others.

*www.jeremyryanslate.com/sharma*

Strategic leaders have to get four tasks. Whether they are in uniform or the CEO of Amazon or Netflix or Alibaba. It's the same for the most senior leaders in the military, the commander of forces in Iraq or Afghanistan, or some of the other very senior organizations in our military ranks.

As a strategic leader, you've got to get the big ideas. You have to get the strategy right, and that's not always all that easy. Petraeus recalls that prior to the surge in Iraq, the military wasn't making progress because we didn't have the right strategy. It became invalidated and it was very difficult to change it.

It took changing the Secretary of Defense and some other key people, including the commander, to change strategy, in what came to be known as the surge. It involves communicating throughout the breadth and depth of the organization. One has to oversee the implementation.

One has to drive the campaign. This is what we normally think of as leadership. This is someone providing the example, the energy, and the sheer will, the determination. It's how the leader spends his or her time. It's the metrics to tell you whether you're winning or losing, making progress or falling behind. It's hiring and firing.

## Extraordinary Fact

- Over 10,000 baby boomers retire every day.
- A whopping 79% of employees will quit their jobs due to lack of appreciation from leaders.
- 69% of Millennials believe there is a lack of leadership development in the workplace.
- Only 15% of women have board of director roles in the workplace.
- 91% of Millennials will stay in their jobs for fewer than three years
- 83% of enterprises believe it's important to develop leaders at all levels in a company.
- Only 5% of companies have integrated leadership development in their corporations.[20]

---

20. Djurovic, Ana, *22 Inspiring Leadership Statistics for a Successful 2022*, 2020, https://goremotely.net/blog/leadership-statistics/

It's promoting those who deserve it. It's allowing those to leave who shouldn't continue. It's all of that kind of activity, which again, we normally associate with the tactics, techniques, and procedures of leadership.

The great leaders, whether in uniform or in the private sector, have invariably performed those four tasks. Most importantly of all, really the absolute most important thing, is to get the big ideas right. That's the element of strategic judgment, and it's an intangible quality.

It's knowing whether you should turn right or left, go straight, or to invest more here and to fold up that; all of these are fundamental decisions impacting the direction of an enterprise. That's really the essence of leadership, because if one doesn't get those right, it doesn't matter how eloquent you are, what a great communicator you may be, how inspirational, energetic, driven, hardworking, focused, all these other capabilities that are so important. If you didn't get the big ideas right in the first place, everything else is built on a shaky intellectual foundation; it's that crucial.

## Extraordinary Takeaway

Leadership can be a difficult topic for many. It's something that has come up many times in my discussion on the podcast. I have found far too often that people who insist on having the title of leader are men and women that do not actually lead. It is those that have humbled themselves and work on themselves every single day that actually have the right to lead others, because those they lead actually respect them.

When it comes down to it, real leadership is about having others respect you so much that they will follow you and listen to your authority. A real leader does not lead out of fear, because eventually fear-driven leadership will consume the leader himself. If you watch throughout all of history, those that have led by fear have seen that fear become anger, and anger is how the populist takes them out.

It's like my friend Eric Rogell says, "It is one who can carry himself as a *king*, a benevolent one, who makes decisions because of their care for the well-being of others, who is a true leader. A true leader figures out how to put the interests of those he leads above his own." This is the reason why people like playing with Tom Brady. He makes them better. It's the reason why people liked playing with Michael Jordan. He made them better. It's the reason people followed Charlemagne. He made his people better.

Leaders have a responsibility for leading those who follow them to a better future than the one they currently have—not one of less freedom, not one of control, but a future for the betterment of mankind. Moving forward, figure out for yourself what leading this planet to be a better place looks like. That first move may be a small one. Or maybe you're in a sector already that requires you to have substantial leadership abilities. do Whatever that thing is that you must do, bravely and courageously go towards it. When it comes down to it, real leaders understand that they are the last line of defense. There is no one else. A leader does not shrug off leadership, but rather, they handle what needs to be done and do not leave it for others. So lead now, and the future will be yours.

# 12. Finding Your Extraordinary

*We're going to relentlessly chase perfection,*
*knowing we will not attain it. Because perfection*
*is unattainable. We're going to relentlessly chase*
*it because in the process we will catch excellence.*

— Vince Lombardi

When it comes down to it, being extraordinary is like a kaleido-scope. Better yet, it's like a mosaic. It takes small pieces of a large collection of skills that we work on every single day. We find ourselves every day trying to be more courageous or working on how we can be a leader.

There are other days where the opinions of others matter more to us than they should, and because of that we make less of ourselves. Finding your extraordinary is not a place you arrive at; rather, it is something that has worked on a daily basis. There will be good days, there will be bad days, but with an eye towards the future, you won't be so stuck in the present.

To be extraordinary is to be able to look into the future when others are stuck in the moments of today—what this politician wants or what this athlete is complaining about. In the grand scheme of things, many of those issues don't really matter. Sure, we should worry about issues that affect our liberty, that goes back to leadership, but we should not dwell on the arguments made in the halls of Congress.

Being extraordinary is not just knowing you're meant for more; it is figuring out how you can reach that more in spite of the losses. Then, once you reach that more, setting a bigger goal so you can continue to grow.

To be extraordinary is to realize that life is not the same forever. You're either growing or you're dying. Extraordinary individuals know that they must focus on growing or the process of living will take care of the dying for them. We all have a finite amount of time on this rock they call Earth. The equalizer is none of us know how long that actually is. That is why I believe to be extraordinary is to live every day as if it's your last. On your last day, will you leave things half done and done poorly? Or will you move forward, create a little mess on the way there, and create greatness? I choose the latter. I hope you do as well.

We've covered, in-depth, the tenants of what it means to be extraordinary. Now that you have a full conceptual understanding of them, let's review the core elements of an extraordinary life.

## Courage

Courage is something we all have. It's something we can't buy more of; it's only something we can build. We do that by taking risks and becoming uncomfortable. It's doing those things that scare us. It's trying those things we are not sure we will like. Courage is something that allows us to lead others. It's that thing that lets us, just as those before us have done, venture off into the great unknown, in spite of peril, to create a future.

## Your Mo Lewis Moment

May you always prepare for when that moment eventually comes. For it will come, just as the seasons change. It is the one who prepares, it is the one who can improve daily, who will be ready when opportunity strikes. As Abraham Lincoln stated, *"I will prepare and my day will come."*

## Don't Follow Your Passion

The best in the world know that their path to greatness is an experience, not just learning. It's the hard-fought School of Hard Knocks where you can learn the things that create the most money. Following your passion is not the best idea. Follow what you're good at, continue to get better at it and better at it and better at it. Once you get to that point where it becomes effortless, that's where the passion comes in, and that's where you can actually create greatness.

## Learn from Failure

Quitters never win, and winners never quit. If you do not allow failure to be final, then you are not a loser. Is it okay to lose if you make it a one-time thing by learning from it. Nick Swisher used the perceived loss of not being drafted out of high school and eventually got drafted from college. You too have an opportunity to create greatness from things that others perceive as losses. Learn to see the opportunity in everything. Then, you can truly be extraordinary.

## Done is Better Than Perfect

Being perfect is the enemy of achievement. When everything must be perfect, nothing ever gets done. Focus on getting moving and cleaning up the mess later. Often perfection leads to advancement whereas perfectionism leads to stagnation. Figure out how you can continue to move forward, even if it's not always pretty. Done is better than perfect.

## Creating Your Own Opportunities

We can't just wait for life to come to us. Sometimes we have to seize the moment, and make that moment into an opportunity. Very few shots are going to come along in life, and you have to be willing to create your own shots. Just like MBA player LeBron James oh, you recognize the moment you pick your spot and you take the shot. Only when you're willing to create opportunities for yourself to win, will you truly win.

## Define Your Own Success

Remember: many of the people who are telling you how to live your life would never die for you. Therefore, you should not live for them. Don't change your life or your plans because of what others think about it. Make decisions based on what you want and what you believe in. Your purpose should not be to make others wrong, but don't stagnate your own success because others fear it.

## Have a Future Vision

If you're going to build your dream, have something to pay the bills, whether that be a job or another business that happened to work out. Have something to pay the bills so you can look at the future. When you're stuck in the past after you've failed, or in the present, trying to make it go right, then you can't look at the future. Find something to fund your now so you can build your future.

## You Have a Duty to Lead

In a world full of sheep, it is the duty of the sheepdogs to prevent what can happen. It is loss of liberty that occurs when others stop caring. If you are able and aware, you have a responsibility to lead others. Lead them into a brighter future, not into a darker tomorrow. To truly appreciate leadership, it is important to see it as a duty and an honor.

## Tell Your Story

Everyone who ever told you it's rude to talk about yourself was wrong. There's nothing wrong with talking about your own achievements or the achievements of your business. In fact, if you don't, no one else will. In a world with so many messages out there, it's very easy to get drowned out. Knowing that, you have to be the one to spread the good news about what you do. Be the evangelist for your brand, telling everyone what you stand for, the impact you're making, and how you can help them.

## Be Radically Responsible

Being fully responsible for your own life is both the scariest thing to learn and the most empowering thing to learn. Once you realize that every single thing that happens to you is because of you, then you know you can change it. When things just happen to you or you're the victim, there's nothing you can do to change your circumstances. Start figuring out how you can be more responsible for your life and the things that happen to you, and you'll find things stop happening to you but start happening because of you.

## To Your Greatness

My friend, all I want for you is greatness. All I want for you is an extraordinary life. In our time together here we've looked at stories of inspiration, of loss, of hard work, and of joy. Don't make this another book that you've just read and moved on from. Make this the change that you need to move forward to become the best version of yourself. To become extraordinary.

May your achievements be great. May your future be bright.

May one day I write a book about you.

Be extraordinary.

# Extraordinary Reads

Reading has been a vital part of my life and personal growth. The following appendix includes books that have given me great insight. I include these books here in hopes you may also get some insight from them too.

The list is not ranked in any particular way; rather, I listed them in the order they came to mind. I tend to get the most insight from biographies and autobiographies, as well as a few select personal-development books. I also tend to read a lot from the same author if I find something valuable in his or her material.

1. *The 10X Rule* – Grant Cardone
2. *American General* – General Tommy Franks
3. *John Adams* – David McCullough
4. *Ermengard of Narbonne and the World of the Troubadours* – Frederic L. Cheyette
5. *Dianetics, The Modern Science of Mental Health* – L. Ron Hubbard
6. *From Alexander to Actium* – Peter Heather
7. *Onward* – Howard Schultz
8. *Atlas Shrugged* – Ayn Rand
9. *The Fountainhead* - Ayn Rand
10. *The Federalist Papers* – Alexander Hamilton, John Jay & James Madison
11. *Steve Jobs* - Walter Isaacson
12. *Crime and Punishment* – Fyodor Dostoyevsky

13. *The Great Bridge* – David McCullough
14. *Brand Intervention* – David Brier
15. *Giftology* – John Ruhlin
16. *Choose Yourself* – James Altucher
17. *Elon Musk* – Ashlee Vance
18. *The Everything Store* – Brad Stone
19. *Shoe Dog* - Phil Knight
20. *Sam Walton* – John Huey & Sam Walton
21. *The Borgias* – G.J. Meyer
22. *The Medici* – Paul Strathern
23. *Belichick* – Ian O'Connor
24. *Ten Caesars* – Barry Strauss
25. *The Captain* – Ian O'Connor
26. *The End is Always Near* – Dan Carlin
27. *The Closer* – Mariano Rivera & Jon Curry
28. *Drive* – Kelley Earnhardt Miller
29. *The Confessions of an Economic Hit Man* – John Perkins
30. *12* – Casey Sherman & Dave Wedge
31. *That First Season* – John Eisenberg
32. *In the Garden of Beasts* – Erik Larsen

# About the Author

Jeremy Ryan Slate is the host of the *Create Your Own Life Podcast*, which studies the highest performers in the world. He studied literature at Oxford University, and holds a Master's in Early Roman Empire Propaganda from Seton Hall University. His podcast was named the #1 Podcast to Listen To by *INC Magazine* in 2019, as well as Top 40 Under 40 by *Podcast Magazine* in 2022.

Jeremy and his wife, Brielle, co-founded Command Your Brand—a new media public relations agency designed to help entrepreneurs share their message by appearing as guests on podcasts. He resides in Stillwater, NJ and is a former competitive powerlifter.

# A free ebook edition is available with the purchase of this book.

**To claim your free ebook edition:**

1. Visit MorganJamesBOGO.com
2. Sign your name CLEARLY in the space
3. Complete the form and submit a photo of the entire copyright page
4. You or your friend can download the ebook to your preferred device

A **FREE** ebook edition is available for you or a friend with the purchase of this print book.

_____

CLEARLY SIGN YOUR NAME ABOVE

**Instructions to claim your free ebook edition:**
1. Visit MorganJamesBOGO.com
2. Sign your name CLEARLY in the space above
3. Complete the form and submit a photo of this entire page
4. You or your friend can download the ebook to your preferred device

## Print & Digital Together Forever.

Snap a photo

Free ebook

Read anywhere